D1388237

Solution-Focused Therapy

Brief Therapies Series

Series Editor: Stephen Palmer
Associate Editor: Gladeana McMahon

Focusing on brief and time-limited therapies, this series of books is aimed at students, beginning and experienced counsellors, therapists and other members of the helping professions who need to know more about working with the specific skills, theories and practices involved in this demanding but vital area of their work.

SOLUTION-FOCUSED THERAPY

Bill O'Connell

SAGE Publications
London • Thousand Oaks • New Delhi

 SAGE Publications Ltd
6 Bonhill Street
London EC2A 4PU

SAGE Publications Inc
2455 Teller Road
Thousand Oaks, California 91320

SAGE Publications India Pvt Ltd
32, M-Block Market
Greater Kailash – I
New Delhi 110 048

British Library Cataloguing in Publication Data

A catalogue record for this book is available
from the British Library

ISBN 0 7619 5274 8
ISBN 0 7619 5275 6 (pbk)

Library of Congress catalog record available

Typeset by Mayhew Typesetting, Rhayader, Powys
Printed in Great Britain by Biddles Ltd, *www.biddles.co.uk*

To Moira, *cariad*

Contents

Foreword

Solution-Focused Therapy is a form of brief therapy that was first developed in the United States in the 1980s. It made its entrance into the UK at the end of the 1980s, and since then thousands of therapists and counsellors in statutory and non-statutory services here have been attracted to short training courses in learning how to use the deceptively simple methods of the approach. A similar movement is taking place across Europe, with therapists in Sweden, Germany, France, Belgium and other countries defining their principal approach as solution-focused brief therapy.

There are of course many different reasons why this therapy has become so popular at this time. Among its attractions, to judge by evaluation forms from training courses, is not only the practical nature of the techniques but also its client-centredness, specifically its focus on competency and strength in clients rather than their assumed deficits and pathology. There seems to be a growing move towards working in partnership with clients, to help them establish what they want to be different in their lives and to seek out the strengths they have for accomplishing those changes. This therefore fits well with research which shows that clients, when asked for their opinion on what helps them in therapy, refer most often to a relationship of trust in which they feel heard – and what better way to develop that than to focus the therapy on what the *client* wants?

It is therefore a pleasure to welcome a valuable addition to the growing collection of writings worldwide which reflect the use of solution-focused therapy. It is doubly pleasing to welcome a book as clear and well written as Bill O'Connell's. Throughout he offers the reader short, readable examples of different facets of the approach that make the material as accessible as possible. In particular he is able to present complex ideas about the background to the approach in a straightforward and succinct manner.

O'Connell tells us that he comes from an eclectic background, and this is demonstrated in his arguments for an integrated approach. Many readers will find his chapter on 'Solution-Focused Therapy and Eclecticism' to be of great value in the way it makes connections between solution-focused brief therapy and other counselling approaches. It teems with useful tips from different approaches and will have something for most people. He also has interesting things to say about adapting the ideas to other settings, such as groups and organisations (see Chapter 10, 'Applications of SFT'), and his chapter on 'Questions Frequently Asked' (Chapter 8) offers some clear and convincing replies to thorny issues.

With his years of practising and teaching counselling skills, it is perhaps inevitable that O'Connell is particularly astute in describing the ingredients of the relationship between therapist and client that are most conducive to a brief approach. Those working as counsellors will find this book, and Chapter 6 in particular, of especial relevance to their work.

The reason, I would guess, that you are holding this book, is because you are interested in brief approaches to therapy that have the aim of empowering clients to take control of their own problem solving abilities. You will find suggestions and strings-to-your-bow aplenty here!

Harvey Ratner
Brief Therapy Practice, London

Preface

This book is intended as an introduction to solution-focused therapy (SFT) for counsellors, social workers, psychologists, nurses and others engaged in the caring professions. It presents solution-focused ideas and practices from a counsellor's point of view. As well as being an introductory handbook, it raises many of the wider issues which any model of therapy must face – its pedigree, its philosophy, its relation to other therapies and its ethical base. Some readers may choose to start with the chapters which cover the practical aspects of the therapy, namely Chapters 3, 4, 5 and 6. Chapter 1 puts the model into the historical context of brief therapy and Chapter 2 provides a theoretical background. Solution-focused supervision is the subject of Chapter 7, while in Chapter 8 I have attempted to answer a series of questions, some of them critical objections to the model. Chapter 9 examines how SFT could integrate with other models, and in Chapter 10 I describe how the model could be used in a variety of settings.

Throughout, I have alternated the use of female and male pronouns, hopefully in a way which avoids gender stereotyping. I have also used the terms counselling/therapy and counsellor/therapist interchangeably, in accordance with the practice of the British Association for Counselling (1996).

The Latin root of the word solution is *solvere*, the verb to release. In that sense, I like to think of SFT as a form of 'liberation therapy', an experience which enables people to release themselves from the tyranny of their pasts. I also like to think that it releases therapists to treat their clients as equal human beings and to affirm and celebrate all that is best about people. On the other hand, there are overtones to the title *Solution-Focused Therapy* which give the impression that there is a solution for every problem, and this leads its critics to dismiss it as a 'quick fix' therapy. For me, a title such as 'Change-Focused Therapy', or

'Future-Oriented Therapy', would be preferable. O'Hanlon (1995) describes his version of solution-oriented therapy as 'Possibility Therapy'.

I also understand the suspicion which many people in the field share towards new forms of brief therapy which conveniently provide a rationale for funders to cut therapy budgets. However, the research base for brief therapy is strong and the reality on the ground is that a lot of the counselling/therapy offered in the UK is actually brief, namely under twenty sessions. Many job specifications for counsellors now require, as an essential, proficiency in brief therapy. Despite this, many counselling training courses fail to train their students in the specific attitudes and skills required to work briefly.

It is not only the funders who are promoting brief therapy but also the clients themselves, who are saying that they benefit from time-limited help and prefer it to a long-term commitment. Provided that brief therapy is not the only treatment option sanctioned, I take the view that practitioners who want to make the best possible use of resources and to extend their distribution to clients currently denied them, should welcome the advent of brief therapy. I believe we need to offer our clients a service which is congruent with their circumstances and preferences, and we need to be accountable to them and to the wider community for the effectiveness of what we do.

I would also like to say that this book is only one practitioner's view of SFT. Having had the opportunity to see presentations by most of the 'gurus' in the field, there is no doubt in my mind that each person customises the model according to his or her previous expertise and background. Many of the American advocates have a background in team-based family therapy, whereas my experience is mainly with individual clients and couples. I have used the model with a wide range of clients in various settings: a student counselling service, a voluntary agency, private practice and two Employee Assistance Programmes. Prior to encountering SFT, my work was heavily influenced by the writing of Gerard Egan and I was always excited by the values and ways of 'being with' a client advocated by Carl Rogers.

Some solution-focused therapists use the model in a 'purist', exclusivist way, while others are more open to integrating it with other models. Coming from an eclectic background, I belong to the latter school and it is my hope that this book will appeal to a broad church of therapists who are open to incorporating new ideas into their practice. This book does not imply criticism of models used by other practitioners, although I would question the need for long-term therapy for all but a minority of clients. The solution-focused principle – 'if it works keep doing it' – is a pragmatic signal to continue with whichever approach you are using if it is working for your clients. However, where it is not working we need to be brave enough to do something else. No therapy always works and the more tools we have in the tool-box, provided we know and understand why we are using them, the better. The state of therapy today encourages us to adopt an eclectic, developmental attitude to our own work. The movement towards consensus and respect for diversity is replacing the sterile polemics of therapy politics and it is in this spirit that the book is written.

I have tried to acknowledge the limitations of the approach as well as its potential. When any form of therapy places a heavy emphasis on certain types of interventions, which means solution-oriented questions in the case of SFT, it inevitably neglects interventions used in other types of therapy. Followers of other therapies will therefore be sensitive to what is not done in SFT as well as surprised at times by what is done. No therapy claims to do everything however, and it is misleading to judge one therapy on the basis of what happens in others. Some critics dismiss SFT because in certain respects it is somewhat lightweight in terms of ideology, but this does not mean that it is simple to practise. It requires the relationship skills needed in all therapies, as well as the ability to focus on what is positive and not problematic about the client, something which many therapists find difficult because it goes against the grain of their training. The novice counsellor, unencumbered by ideas and practices from other schools, may find it easier to practise in a solution-focused way than will the person trained in other models. However, in my opinion, it is beneficial for solution-focused counsellors to have undergone a generalist counselling training first, before they begin to practise in a solution-focused way. This is particularly the case in Europe where, as I understand it, there is no full-length SFT training course. SFT makes no claim to be a superior brand of therapy; it claims the same degree of effectiveness as most other forms of therapy. As well as believing that the model is beneficial for clients, from my experience as a trainer, it is clear that it also has a positive impact on the morale and expertise of the practitioners, some of whom have reported that they believe it has saved them from burn-out. I hope that this book helps readers to enjoy their privileged occupation and to be of greater service to their clients.

Acknowledgements

I would like to express my sincere thanks to those people who made this book possible. In the first place, my warmest thanks go to my wife Moira, my grown-up daughters Donnamarie, Joanne and Katrina for the love and support they have always given me. I also owe a great debt of gratitude to my colleague Janet Bellamy at Westhill College for all her help, and also to Clare Austin and Joyce Colwell. I am especially grateful to the many students and clients who have taught me so much over the years. May I thank John Wheeler for his constructive and informed comments throughout the writing of the book; Harvey Ratner and his colleagues at the Brief Therapy Practice for their encouragement; and Gladeana McMahon, Stephen Palmer and Susan Worsey at Sage for their support.

1

Brief Therapy

Solution-focused therapy (SFT) is a form of brief therapy which emerged in the 1980s from the family therapy tradition in the USA, and in particular from the work of Steve de Shazer and his team at the Brief Family Therapy Center in Milwaukee. Although the context of their work was with families, from the point of view of practitioners who work mainly with individuals it is helpful to see the model in the context of other brief therapy models.

The fact that many brief therapy models are attached to the main schools of therapy (psychodynamic and cognitive behaviour in particular) may give the impression that brief therapy is a derivative of long-term therapy. However, this is not the case. Bloom (1992) lists a large number of case studies over the past eighty years in which patients present as having made significant changes in their lives as a result of brief therapy. Eminent therapists, such as Ferenczi and Rank (1925), have argued against the assumption that analysis had to be lengthy. They advocated that the therapist should adopt an active empathic stance in making interpretations, promoting transference and keeping the emotional temperature high. Rank emphasised the importance of the client's motivation to engage in a process of change, the need to set an end to treatment and the necessity for more attention to be paid to the current experiences of the client rather than a reliving of the past. However, the psychoanalytic community remained defensive and hostile to the idea that therapy which was not lengthy and 'deep' could be of any lasting value. Alexander and French (1946) provoked considerable hostility when they wrote about the 'almost superstitious belief among psychoanalysts that quick therapeutic results cannot be genuine'. They had recommended using weekly rather than daily sessions to enable clients to put into practice what they had learned in therapy.

Malan's influential studies (1963, 1976) demonstrated the efficacy of short-term dynamic therapy. He highlighted the need for careful assessments and the need to retain a therapeutic focus for the work. From the 1960s to the 1980s the works of Malan, Mann (1973) Sifneos (1979) and Davanloo (1980) were the driving forces behind the case for brief dynamic casework. Since then, the increasing body of research demonstrating that brief therapy is equally as effective as long term (summarised in Koss and Butcher 1986), and that brief therapy is the expectation and preference for more than 70 per cent of clients (Garfield and Bergin 1994, Pekarik 1991), has been a powerful market force. Frances, Clarkin and Perry (1984) found that a wide range of practitioners – marital therapists, sex therapists, family therapists, crisis therapists and cognitive-behavioural therapists – all claimed to work within a short period of time and that their actual practice bore this out. One study of a counselling centre in the UK (Brech and Agulnik 1996) found that approximately 40 per cent of clients had between one and four sessions, a further 40 per cent between five and twenty, and 20 per cent had therapy contracts extending beyond six months. The study found that by introducing a four-session model for clients on the waiting list, the number waiting was reduced and this reduced the waiting time for all clients, even those who had not accepted the offer of four sessions and who chose to wait for more open-ended therapy. The majority of studies over recent decades show that the median length of treatment of whatever orientation ranges from four to eight sessions, with a clustering around six (Garfield and Bergin 1994, Koss and Butcher 1986). Koss and Butcher (1986) conclude that 'almost all psychotherapy is brief'.

There are differences in definition as to what constitutes brief therapy. Eckert (1993) defined brief therapy as being 'any psychological intervention intended to produce change as quickly as possible whether or not a specific time limit is set in advance'. Malan (1976), from a psychodynamic tradition, used the term to mean between four and fifty sessions; Mann (1973), from the same tradition, set a fixed number of twelve; while Ryle's (1991) cognitive analytic model used sixteen. Talmon (1990) and Manthei (1996) argue the case for single-session therapy. While some models set fixed limits, others are brief within flexible parameters (Steenbarger 1994). Budman and Gurman (1988) prefer the term 'time-sensitive therapy', which they feel highlights the need for the therapist to make maximum impact within a rationed amount of time. Although there are major differences between brief therapists, there is a degree of consensus that brief therapy means less than twenty sessions.

There is considerable agreement in the literature about the main characteristics of planned brief therapy. These features are also prominent in solution-focused brief therapy. Barret-Kruse (1994) summarises them as:

- the view that self and others are essentially able
- the acceptance of the client's definition of the problem
- the formation of the therapeutic alliance
- the crediting of success to the client
- the therapist learning from the client
- the avoidance of a power struggle with the client
- the objectification, rather than the personalisation, of the client's behaviour.

She asserts that in brief therapy the therapist needs to join with the client to communicate an expectancy of change. This necessitates a mixture of co-operation and directiveness from the therapist in order to enable a working relationship to form as quickly as possible. It is equally important to identify the problem and the goal(s) clearly and to develop appropriate action plans which are carefully evaluated. In brief therapy the client defines the problem. Wells and Gianetti (1993), in emphasising the need to educate clients into their roles, argue that a collaborative and effective relationship can be more quickly established if clients are given as much information about the problem and the therapy as possible. For Bloom (1981) the key question behind brief therapy is: 'What have these clients failed to understand about their lives that could make a difference in how they are conducting themselves now and how they might manage their lives in the future?'

Koss and Butcher (1986) summarise the research by describing the main features of brief therapy as:

- a focus on the here and now
- clear, specific and attainable goals that can be achieved in the time available
- the establishment of a good working relationship as soon as possible

- the projection of the therapist as competent, hopeful and confident
- the therapist is active and openly influential.

In contrast, Hoyt (1995) identifies a number of beliefs which underpin long-term therapy:

- damaging early experiences must be slowly and fully uncovered
- the therapeutic alliance must form gradually
- the client must be allowed to regress
- transference takes a long time to develop and must not be interpreted too early
- consolidation of gains requires a lengthy period of working through.

Effectiveness

The research evidence for the effectiveness of brief therapy is impressive. Kogan (1957) followed up clients three and twelve months after they had received a single session of therapy. Approximately two-thirds felt that they had been helped. He concluded that in cases with unplanned endings, therapists consistently underestimated the help which clients had received. Malan, Heath, Bacal and Balfour (1975), in a study of forty-five clients, two to eight years after they had received a single session of therapy, found that a quarter had improved symptomatically and another quarter had also improved in dynamic terms. Smith (1980) found that the major impact of therapy occurred in the first six to eight sessions, followed by a continuing but decreasing positive impact for approximately the next ten sessions. Howard, Kopta, Krause and Orlinsky (1986), in a meta-study, found that 15 per cent of clients improved before the first session, 50 per cent by the eighth, 75 per cent by the twenty-sixth and 83 per cent by the fifty-second. Stern (1993) suggests that those who stay longer are those who do not feel that they have made enough progress. Brech and Agulnik (1996) found that of clients who received four planned sessions of therapy in a setting which used psychodynamic methods, 25 per cent found it useful and sufficient, and for a further 50 per cent it was a useful beginning which helped them to plan the possibility of further long-term work. Bloom (1992) concluded that short-term psychotherapies were essentially equally as effective as time-unlimited psychotherapy.

Howard and his colleagues' meta-study (1986) suggests that, although frequency of sessions was not related to improvement, the structuring of therapy is important because clients can use regular sessions as organising factors in their lives. It can be helpful to have special times assigned for themselves and in addition there must be a degree of intensity in sessions for change to take place.

It is not clear whether therapy is brief because it works or it works because it is brief. Perry (1987) suggests that the effectiveness of brief therapies may be due to the techniques used, rather than to the short duration of the therapy itself.

In 1990 Talmon published his influential study on single-session therapy. He researched over 10,000 outpatients of a psychiatric hospital who had received psychotherapy. He discovered that the most frequent length of therapy was one session and that 30 per cent of all patients chose to come for only one session in a period of one year, irrespective of the theoretical orientation of the therapist. Moreover, in a follow-up study of 200 of his own clients, 78 per cent said that they had received what they had wanted from one session. In another study of planned single-session therapy he found that 88 per cent of clients reported that they had improved since the first session and 79 per cent thought that the one session had been enough. His study challenged the view that clients who leave therapy early are failed 'drop outs'. He claimed that his research indicated that brief therapy was the preferred choice of many clients and that more therapy need not necessarily mean more effective therapy. As Hoyt (1995: 144) puts it, 'More is not necessarily better. Better is better.'

The limited research on SFT typically uses clients' own perceptions of their progress, a methodology which is consistent with the principles of the therapy itself. Kiser and Nunnally's study (1990) of the Brief Family Therapy Center at Milwaukee, the home of SFT, reported an 80.4 per cent success rate (65.6 per cent of clients met their goals, while 14.7 per cent made significant improvement) within an average of 4.6 sessions. When the clients were recontacted after eighteen months, the success rate had increased to 86 per cent. In a second study of the Center's work, De Jong and Hopwood (1996) found that over three-quarters of clients either fully met their treatment goals or made progress towards them. They also found that the average number of sessions was 2.9.

Consumer preference

Intermittent therapy, which is analogous to visiting a doctor from time to time as and when needed, may be more suited to the way people currently live their lives. Cummings and Sayama (1995) argue for therapy to be intermittent throughout the life cycle. In their opinion, brief focused therapy, which can be resumed at points of crisis during a person's life, is more effective than other models. There is evidence that brief therapy is the therapy of choice for consumers. According to Pekarik and Wierzbicki (1986), long-term therapy (over 15 sessions) was preferred by 65 per cent of therapists in the cases they studied, whereas only 20 per cent of their clients expected it. This may suggest that clients do not see themselves as being entitled to lengthy therapy, although that may be their preference; or it might point to clients not wanting 'to be *in* therapy', but rather choosing to go *through* it as quickly as possible. There is some evidence that clients opt for brief therapy even when they are entitled to have lengthier therapy at no cost to themselves (Hoyt 1995). Such findings have clear implications for the just distribution of scarce therapy resources. Client and therapist experience of the process itself is very different. Llewelyn (1988), for example, found that clients were most interested in gaining a solution to their problems and feeling better, whereas therapists were more concerned with the aetiology of the problem and its transformation through insight. There is also evidence that clients' expectations about outcomes differ from many therapists'. Warner (1996) demonstrated that counsellors find it difficult to believe that clients have benefited from brief interventions. According to Beutler and Crago (1987), the majority of clients are looking for symptom relief whereas their therapists hope to bring about character change. The distinction between these two goals cannot be complete, as the former can lead to the latter and the first signs of character development are likely to be that the client finds new ways of handling his immediate problems. Brief therapy does not mean 'less of the same' but therapy with its own structure and process that differs from long term (Barkham 1993).

2

Foundations of SFT

When the invention of the steam engine was first announced in the last century, a distinguished scientist and wit is reported to have remarked: 'It works in practice, but does it work in theory?'

(quoted in O'Hanlon and Wilk 1987).

The founders of solution-focused therapy (SFT), the team at the Brief Family Therapy Center (BFTC) in Milwaukee, and Steve de Shazer in particular, state that the model evolved from clinical practice (de Shazer, Berg, Lipchik, Nunnally, Molnar, Gingerich and Weiner-Davis 1986). They discovered that their clients were helped just as effectively by engaging in talk about the future as by talking about the problem-laden past. It appeared important to help clients describe what they wanted to have present in their lives (the solution), which was more than just the absence of the problem (non-problem). The solution did not have to fit the problem and could not possibly have emerged from the problem itself, it needed to fit what the client saw to be the desired goal. These 'skeleton keys', as de Shazer (1985) called them, could be used across a range of problems. These formulaic interventions included encouragement to 'do something different', 'look for exceptions to the problem' and 'notice what you would like to see continue in your life' (First Session Formula Task), as well as the use of techniques such as scaling and the miracle question.

The discovery that future-oriented interventions could help clients to find ways out of their problems revolutionised the team's practice. In numerous articles and books, de Shazer described how experimental interventions designed to facilitate solution talk were tested by members of the team (de Shazer 1984, de Shazer 1985, de Shazer and Molnar 1984, de Shazer et al. 1986). Their overriding aim was to discover what worked for the client.

They stayed as close to the client's agenda as possible by developing a strong collaborative relationship and a clear picture of client goals. They encouraged clients to focus on what was changeable and attainable, rather than being daunted and disempowered by the size of the problem. They sought to leave aside labels which the clients or their referrers brought with them and chose to concentrate more on non-problem behaviour, client competence and personal strengths, in the belief that people tend to behave well when treated well, to act competently when they are treated as competent. The BFTC team emphasised the importance of learning from the client how to do therapy. Their reflections on what they were observing and experiencing led them to articulate a philosophical and epistemological basis for it. In this chapter I will attempt to identify the key ideas which shaped SFT. As practitioners from many cultures use it, the action research base is growing and various orientations within the broad school are emerging. Some practitioners are, for example, more open to using solution-focused ideas and techniques within an eclectic framework than others. There is also a growing convergence between some narrative approaches and SFT.

Schwartz (1955) identified three stages through which new theories pass:

1 In the first stage, the Essentialist, there are many competing schools, each claiming superiority. Their followers tend to be evangelical, narrow and intolerant zealots. This stage lasts until the flaws and limitations of the theory appear and/or it becomes integrated into the establishment.
2 In the second stage, the Transitional, the followers themselves begin to recognise limitations to their model and this can result in civil war between the progressives who accept these new insights and the orthodox who 'defend the faith' and see themselves as the true believers. They may retreat into the Essentialist stage. A dialectical tension between the two extremes may produce a centre party.
3 The third stage, which he calls Ecological, is a process of integrating with other ideas, accompanied by an understanding of the constantly evolving nature of the field. In this stage a more eclectic position may emerge.

This sequence of events often applies to new models of therapy as they seek to find their place in an ever busier market-place.

Converts to a new approach to therapy may, like converts to any cause, deter rather than win new devotees by being too strident in their testimony. I hope to avoid this by showing how the practice of SFT can be integrated into the repertoire of therapists, whatever their orientation, and to acknowledge its limitations.

Epistemology

In understanding theories of therapy it is essential to address the philosophical and epistemological positions which 'underlie' them. Lynch (1996) identifies three perspectives on knowledge and reality available to the counsellor and researcher. The first perspective, a modern position, argues that there is an objective reality which we can have an objective knowledge of through the use of reason. This is the stance taken by the scientific/medical model with its emphasis on testing hypotheses by rational analysis of cause and effect. The second perspective, a social constructionist post-modern one, claims that there is no objective meaning to reality and that all meaning is a human creation influenced by social and cultural factors. Since language is a public phenomenon, our knowledge of reality is shaped by the linguistic context in which it is used. What was considered previously as being a definitive version of 'the truth' was actually the dominant discourse of the powerful. Historically in the western world, this meant a white, male, heterosexual viewpoint. Other views of the world, such as black, female, gay, were regarded as deviations from the norm. The post-modern position takes a critical, anti-authoritarian stance towards 'establishment' dogmas. It is pragmatic and pluralistic in its approach. The third perspective, which emphasises context, takes the view that there is an objective order and meaning in reality, but we are unable to know it because we are always constrained by our social context.

Practitioners vary in terms of how aware or committed they are to these epistemological stances. Their lack of awareness does not alter the fact that their practice makes many epistemological assumptions. The current prevalence of pragmatic attitudes within psychotherapy is helpful in that they are more creative than the narrow, defensive and polemical mentality which has characterised much of the history of psychotherapy. However, a failure to pay rigorous attention to theoretical assumptions can lead to a practice which becomes merely technical and divorced from the ideological soil from which it sprang.

SFT belongs to the constructionist school of therapies, included among which are Kelly's personal construct approach (1955), neuro-linguistic programming (Bandler and Grinder 1979), the brief problem-solving model developed at the Mental Research Institute (MRI) in Palo Alto in California by Watzlawick, Weakland and Fisch (1974) and the narrative approach as described by White and Epston (1990). The MRI and the SFT model owed much to the seminal thinking of Gregory Bateson (1972) and Milton Erickson (1980).

Constructionism

In ancient Greece, the word *theoria* referred to a privileged group of male citizens who were allowed to attend ritual cultic events, the athletic games and major public ceremonies. Their report back to the rest of the populace was considered to be 'the truth' about these occasions. Our use of the word 'theory' is as a form of explanation for particular realities – it is a framework for making sense of information. The social constructionist epistemology which underpins SFT would critique the power claimed by the *theoria* to be the one, true interpreter of reality. Constructionism states that meaning is known only through social interaction and negotiation. We have no direct access to objective truth, independent of our linguistically constructed versions of reality. Theories are not objective versions of an external reality, but socially constructed views which emerge within a cultural, political and social context. According to Walter and Peller:

> The implications of seeing meaning-making as a social event of at least two selves while at the same time realizing that language is not tied to an objective reality, are that in a conversation there are at least two stories, at least two constructions, and a mutual, co-ordinated construction process. (1996: 14)

No one person or school of thought possesses more of 'the truth' than another; the therapist does not have access to esoteric truths denied the client.

> The social constructionist values not knowing – knowledge is created out of conversations. There can be no drawing of irrevocable conclusions which are substantiated by selectively gathering and attending to data which support the theory. (Allen 1993: 31)

The knower actively participates in constructing what is observed. According to Segal (1986), constructionism challenges our hopes that reality exists independently of us, the observers, and undermines our wish for reality to be discoverable, predictable and certain. Constructionism claims that this inseparability of the known from the knower destroys the myth of absolute truth and the rigid dogmas which accompany it. Von Foerster's puzzle demonstrates the point by presenting us with a sentence and inviting us to fill in the missing word:

This sentence has . . . letters.

The answer must include itself in the number of letters and there could be different answers depending on which number is chosen. You could not choose any number, as there are already twenty-two letters before you insert your chosen number. In other words, there are different correct answers to the problem (Segal 1986).

Constructionism claims to present us with a much richer, more diverse way of looking at our world – one in which we have greater choices. In the therapeutic encounter there is therefore an extensive repertoire of meanings which the therapist and the client can explore in order to reach an understanding. This does not mean that any explanation for a 'problem' will suffice, but it underlines the subjectivity and cultural relativity of the language we use to describe our realities. Therapy becomes a dialogue in which both partners construct the problem and the solution. It is a language game. The problem does not have an objective, fixed meaning which the clients bring with them. Instead, clients tell and retell their story using language which reshapes the social reality by which they live. In Watzlawick's phrase (1984), 'reality is invented, not discovered'. Language does not simply reflect reality, it creates it.

A structuralist representational view of language has historically dominated therapy. According to it, the task of the therapist is to get 'behind' or 'beneath' the language used by the client in order to discover meaning to the narrative. The tools which the therapist uses depend upon her philosophical and epistemological stance in regard to knowledge, pathology and the nature of the human person. In the structural approach to language there is a belief that language represents 'real' things out there, which have an objectivity independently of us knowing them – for example, personality, behaviour, self-esteem. The trained therapist's task is to help the client find this lost 'truth' which will confer meaning on the client's experience. The enlightenment arising from this discovery will hopefully guide and motivate the client into living more resourcefully. The quest for the 'truth' of the client's life will take different paths according to whether the therapist believes that the key to the door lies in identifying repressed damaging experiences from the past, faulty irrational beliefs, learned maladaptive behaviour or lack of self-actualisation. On the journey, the therapist gathers evidence which will either confirm or challenge the original hypothesis. At some stage, the therapist will share this 'evidence' with the client, who will either accept or reject it. If the client owns this discovery both parties feel as if they have stumbled upon something 'real' which was waiting there, hidden but discoverable. They will have created a 'common vantage point from which to survey the world together' (Taylor 1985). Russell (1989: 505) describes this as a 'public space in which the character of social/physical realities are crafted and essayed linguistically'. The newly acquired knowledge will hopefully prove valuable to the client in understanding and changing the problem situation.

Figure 2.1 highlights many of the key qualities of a form of constructionism which focuses on the social context of language. These qualities are as follows:

- Constructionism gives precedence to the client's perceptions and experiences, rather than to 'the facts'.
- It utilises the multiplicity of narratives which clients could choose in order to bring about the changes they want.
- It emphasises the importance of 'joining with' the client in order to co-create a new and empowering narrative.
- It invites the therapist to affirm the expertise and unique experience of the client and to disown a privileged position of knowledge and power.
- It pays attention to the context in which the client's narrative developed. This increases its potential for respecting and working with difference.
- It acknowledges the competence and strengths of people.
- It demands that the counsellor develop a clear sense of her own values, 'blind spots' and biases.

Attributes of social constructionism (SC)	*Non-attributes*
SC provides a conceptual context for understanding the counselling relationship	SC is not a new type of therapy or even a set of therapeutic techniques
SC deals with theory, personal accounts, and other evidence in terms of its usefulness rather than in terms of truth or external validity	SC is not a licence for saying all views are equally legitimate or persuasive
SC recognises that individuals will have preferences for particular ways of viewing experiences etc.	SC does not accept that these personal choices constitute truth or reality statements
SC proposes that personal knowledge derives from participation in social interaction via participation in conversation and social exchange, and holds that problems are generated by and embedded in current patterns of meaning and interaction rather than being products of inside (the individual) or outside factors	SC is not a restriction requiring that the counsellor does not hold a view, nor that references to social structures, social 'realities' and individual characteristics cannot be made
SC proposes that instructive interaction cannot have a certain outcome, i.e. what the 'expert' tells the 'non-expert' does not determine what the non-expert then comes to believe, know or do	SC does not require that the counsellor never assumes an expert role or relationship with the client
SC supports the view that counselling is constructive rather than remedial	SC is not consistent with a view that counselling repairs faulty people or social systems
SC is dependent on the ability and willingness of the counsellor to remain non-attached to rules, structures and personal preferences in order to be free to consider and propose other ways of describing what appears to be happening	SC does not require that the counsellor remains personally neutral or passive to the information received
SC seeks to understand the concepts, rules and structures of the client's experiences and story	SC is not preoccupied with the construction of explanatory or causal schema
Understanding is always interpretative since SC insists there is no privileged standpoint for understanding	SC is not simply a reframing of people's accounts with 'superior' versions

Figure 2.1   *Social Constructionism (Street and Downey, 1996: 121, reprinted with permission)*

There are some major assumptions which traditional therapy often makes:

1   Western thinking tends to assume that there is a necessary connection between a problem and its solution. The solution should look like the problem. If, for example, the client has had a problem for a long time it is commonly thought that it will take a long time for a solution to emerge. If the problem is complex, then it is thought that the solution will also be complex. SFT challenges such assumptions by demonstrating that clients can be helped without in-depth exploration of the problem and by arguing that the solution construction process is separable from the problem construction process.

2   Associations between events are often viewed as being causally connected. In the psychological realm these connections are frequently tenuous and unprovable. Is someone depressed because he has a genetic predisposition towards depression, and/or because his family life was disrupted when his parents' marriage split up when he was ten, and/or he lacked the social skills and confidence to make close relationships, and /or he has low self-esteem, and/or he is long-term unemployed? How are we to weigh up those factors? How do we know they are true? How do we know when we have gone 'deep' enough? Where does the therapist start to work on an agenda as diffuse as this? How long is it going to take for change to take place? As Segal (1986) states, in his discussion of the work of Von Foerster, we are obsessed with efficient causality, a form of explanation in which the cause precedes the effect. Most forms of therapy function by seeking causal mechanisms for the current problems in the client's life. But there are other forms of causality, and SFT attaches greater importance to final causality, where the effect precedes the cause. This focuses attention on how our future goals shape what we do in the present. If we have greater clarity about our preferred future it will motivate and clarify what we need to do in the present. An analogy would be a journey in which the driver or pilot works back from the time at which the car or plane should arrive at its destination, to plot the course, speed, amount of fuel and stopping-off places along the way. The end point determines the means. In engineering, manufacturers examine and dismantle their

competitor's product, such as a car engine, in order to work out how it was made. In therapy, we can look with the client at the end 'product', then work back to find out how the client might get there. Instead of clients becoming trapped in trying to analyse why they are stuck, they harness the energy and dynamism inherent in the solution.

3 There is often an assumption made by therapists that x has to happen before y can happen. For example, that the client must learn to express emotions before she will be able to resume a normal life. There is an assumption that one must fully understand the problem before being able to resolve it, otherwise improvement will only be temporary. There is an assumption that the 'deeper' the psychic investigation the more 'truthful' the findings will be. There is an assumption that change lies in the revealing of explanatory mechanisms. Without wishing to deny the importance of understanding and insight, I suggest that understanding does not guarantee change and that change does not guarantee understanding.

The therapist uses a psychological map which enables her to explore the terrain with the client. The 'realist' believes that the map is a true or accurate representation of a landscape 'out there' (although the terrain is actually intra-psychic). In engaging with the therapist in a map-reading exercise, the aim is for the client to reach an understanding of the origins of the obstacles in her path and, armed with that knowledge, be able to overcome them. Therapy comes to an end when the client is sufficiently on the right road. The therapist tends to be seen as the expert guide who knows the short cuts and the pitfalls along the way. The chosen route depends upon the kind of journey which the two parties jointly negotiate. Some may prefer the long way round, others the shortest route between two points.

In SFT the meaning of the client's experiences is seen as negotiable and dependent upon the outcome of the linguistic transactions in which the client and therapist engage. The therapist adopts a 'not knowing' position in which she disowns the role of expert, 'the keeper of the truth', in the client's life. The purpose of the therapeutic dialogue is to negotiate jointly a meaning to the client's situation which will create the possibility of change for him. If problem talk disempowers the client, the therapist challenges it by attempting to use other discourses which are potentially more open to change. We use language to construct and deconstruct our own changing reality.

Negotiating narratives with clients is the essence of any type of therapy. In the solution-focused approach, certain types of narrative are seen as more likely to motivate and support a client towards change than others. These are narratives about competence, skills and qualities which the client can utilise. They are also narratives about the future, more than the past. Future-oriented talk challenges the client's belief that the future will only be more of the past. History can be renegotiated in order to learn from it. When driving a car it can be useful to look occasionally in the rear mirror, but it is advisable to spend most of the time looking through the front windscreen!

The MRI model

The MRI brief therapy problem-focused model views problems as developing because people establish patterns of interaction in relation to a difficulty which do not actually resolve it. These patterns may include under-reacting to the problem by avoiding or denying it, or by taking actions which either have little effect or even compound the problem. The problem becomes the sum of the failed solutions.

Practitioners from the MRI school (Weakland and Jordan 1992: 245) describe clearly how clients repeat failed solutions:

1   The client uses more of the same type of 'solution' and only varies the performance slightly by, for example, turning up the volume or increasing the frequency.
2   The client avoids doing something which needs to be done. The client may not be able to summon the energy/the effort to do what she knows needs to be done.
3   Clients act in ways which are irrelevant or inappropriate to the problem, the 'moving deck chairs on the Titanic' syndrome. They may engage in strategies, such as overworking, in order to prevent them having to think about the problem.
4   The client tries to go two ways at once. In desperation, the client may chase solutions in opposite directions which cancel each other out – for example, fasting and bingeing.
5   Looking for the perfect solution. 'Attempts to do the impossible in actuality will prevent doing what is possible

and desirable, and will also make what might otherwise be bearable appear intolerable because it is imperfect' (Weakland and Jordan 1992: 245).

The therapist needs to identify and explore the vicious circles which surround the problem and find ways of getting the client to act to interrupt the problem cycle. It is important to clarify precisely why the client has come for therapy and what exactly she hopes to gain from it. This, as any practitioner will know, is not always easy, as clients can be vague and unsure about the nature of the problem and ambivalent about what they hope to achieve from therapy. The therapist also tries to discover what the client or other significant people are doing to maintain the problem. Clients are encouraged to set clear, specific, small, but realistic, goals. The aim of these strategies is to displace the failed attempted solution by either disrupting the status quo and/or by encouraging a quite different way of looking at or acting upon the problem. Clients are usually given tasks to be performed between sessions.

The focus of the work is on clients' presenting problems and not on underlying issues. 'The presenting problem offers, in one package, what the patient is ready to work on, a concentrated manifestation of whatever is wrong, and a concrete index of any progress made' (Weakland, Fisch, Watzlawick and Bodin 1974: 147).

Both the MRI and the SFT model were influenced by the innovatory work of Milton Erickson, 'the father of Strategic therapy'. According to Lankton (1990), the characteristics of Erickson's therapy were:

- *A non-pathology model* Problems result from a limited repertoire of behaviours and attitudes on the part of clients.
- *Indirection* The therapist helps clients to tap into resources of which they were unaware, without the role of the therapist interfering.
- *Utilisation* This consists of mobilising any aspect of the client's experience which could usefully contribute to resolving the problem.
- *Action* The therapist expects clients to act outside the therapy sessions to make the changes they want.
- *Strategic* The therapist designs interventions specifically for each client.

- *Future-oriented*   The emphasis is on the future, more than on the past or present.
- *Enchantment*   The therapy seeks to engage clients in ways which appear attractive to them.

Most of these principles are found in SFT, although therapist-designed strategic interventions are rarely used. Instead, the therapist trusts the client's best instincts and sees the client as creative, imaginative and resourceful. The therapist too is optimistic, hopeful, creative and imaginative. She helps the client to keep going in the direction of his goals but is not the expert who knows or chooses what that direction should be.

The epistemological basis of SFT offers the therapist a rich and varied access into the client's world. Its sensitivity to the power of language in socially constructing the problem creates many possible therapeutic conversations. Its acknowledgement of the presence of many different 'truths' and standpoints validates the world view of clients, while providing a basis for 'reauthoring' (White 1995) the client's narrative. Its recognition of the social context of language highlights the powerful impact of culture, race and gender discourses in therapy. It offers a model of the therapist–client relationship characterised by respect for the client's expertise. Its reluctance to reify problems into fixed and defined 'truths' about clients highlights the dynamic process of change and increases the possibility of change.

3

Overview of the Model

There's nothing wrong with you that what's right with you couldn't fix.

Baruch Shalem

Solution-focused therapy (SFT) has been used with a wide range of problems: mental illness (Wilgosh 1993), alcohol abuse (Berg and Miller 1992), violence (Lipchik 1991), sexual abuse (Dolan 1991), marital conflicts (Hudson and O'Hanlon 1991), parenting and school difficulties (Durrant 1993b, Lethem 1994, Rhodes and Ajmal 1995). It is interesting to note that the Brief Family Therapy Center in Milwaukeee was, and still is, a non-profit-making service for clients from socially deprived areas. It could be that SFT, with its respect for the strengths of the client and its rich descriptive language which avoids abstractions, is more user-friendly to people in lower socio-economic groups. It may be more suited to the restricted language code of many people, as described by Bernstein (1972).

Although SFT is designed to be brief, and in practice often is, this need not always be the case. It is not time limited in the sense of offering contracts for a fixed number of sessions. De Shazer (1996) reports that, on average, clients at the BFTC attend for three sessions. Cade and O'Hanlon (1993) state that therapy should end as soon as is respectfully possible. As Miller (1994) points out, SFT cannot claim to be briefer than other methods as research has consistently shown that clients on average attend for four to six sessions (Koss and Butcher 1986) regardless of the model employed. However, as we have seen, there are certain principles and methods which, if followed, are more likely to make therapy brief.

SFT adopts the principle of minimal intervention. Following Occam's axiom that 'it is vain to do with more what can be achieved with fewer', SFT makes the fewest assumptions necessary to explain the client's situation (Cade and O'Hanlon 1993). They argue that the analysis of ideas and repetitive sequences surrounding 'symptoms' is a sufficient level of explanation for engaging in therapy:

> Brief Therapy is primarily concerned with observable phenomena, is pragmatic and believes that problems are produced and maintained by the constructs through which difficulties are viewed and by repetitive behavioural sequences surrounding them, including the constructs and inputs of therapists. (Cade and O'Hanlon 1993: 5)

They further suggest that minimal interference reduces the dangers of unduly prolonging therapy and thereby creating a sense of dependency in clients. As well as helping to keep therapy brief while respecting the uniqueness of each client, minimal theoretical assumptions discourage classifying, categorizing or speculating about the problem. A feature of the minimal intervention approach is the reluctance of the solution-focused therapist to take a case history in the orthodox sense, or to formulate an explanation for the client's difficulties. Fisch (1994) suggests that the more explanatory data sought ('Why' questions), as distinct from descriptive data ('What did you do next?'), the more prolonged therapy is likely to be. Explanatory data encourage elaboration by both therapist and client into speculative discourse ('I think he's been like this since I started going out to work, but on the other hand he was having a lot of problems when his father left us'). Another reason why therapy is more likely to be brief is that the therapist focuses on the complaint brought by the client and does not stray into other areas of the client's life. The solution-focused therapist does not regard therapy as a definitive, once-in-a-lifetime experience, but as a supportive event which enables the client to initiate a process of ongoing change.

Problem-focused v. solution-focused

Figure 3.1 compares a problem-focused and a solution-focused approach. The therapist would not necessarily verbalise these questions but they will influence his thinking. The model is an oversimplification designed to highlight differences. It does not imply that talking about the problem or about the past is

Problem-focused	Solution-focused
• How can I help you?	• How will you know that therapy has been helpful?
• Could you tell me about the problem?	• What would you like to change?
• Is the problem a symptom of something deeper?	• Have we clarified the central issue on which you want to concentrate?
• Can you tell me more about the problem?	• Can we discover exceptions to the problem?
• How are we to understand the problem in the light of the past?	• What will the future look like without the problem?
• What defence mechanisms are operating?	• How can we use the skills and qualities of the client?
• In which ways is the relationship between the therapist and the client a replay of past relationships? (psychodynamic models?)	• How can the therapist collaborate with the client?
• How many sessions will be needed?	• Have we achieved enough to end?

Figure 3.1   *A comparison between a problem-focused and a solution-focused approach*

anathema in SFT. However, the perspective taken on the past is rather different than from most other forms of therapy. The figure is not intended to suggest that there is a stark choice between each form of question – therapy is never as neat and tidy.

How can I help you? v. How will you know that therapy is helpful?
The introductory phrases used by the therapist indicate how she sees the process of therapy. The former stresses the expert role, the 'privileged position' of the therapist, and implies that she can provide something which the client cannot give or do for himself. The second question emphasises what the client hopes to achieve and how he will know when he has achieved it. As far as possible, the end of therapy is sketched out from the beginning. If the client is able to answer this question there is a greater chance therapy will be effective. Finding out what the client wants

- How long do you think it will take before things get better?
- How many times do you expect we will need to meet?
- How will you know that it has been worth your while to come here today?
- How do you think therapy might help you?
- How will you know when things are getting better?

Figure 3.2   *Goal-oriented questions*

actively recruits him as an equal partner in a joint enterprise. Figure 3.2 suggests some questions which might be used.

Could you tell me about the history of the problem? v. What would you like to change?

Kelly (1955) said, 'if you do not know what is wrong with a person, ask him; he may tell you'. This is a useful reminder of the importance of the client's construction of the problem and a warning against the imposition of a problem/solution framework by the therapist. A problem-focused approach gathers as much information as possible about the patterns of problem behaviour in order to design an intervention which will break the problematic vicious circle. A solution-focused approach will spend less time on the past and more on a description of the kind of future the client wants. This question, which is likely to appear in some form in the first interview, invites the client to describe the specific behaviours he wants to alter and sets a climate of expectancy about change. It implies that the client has the potential to make changes and is motivated to do so.

Is the problem a symptom of something deeper? v. Have we agreed the central issue on which you want to concentrate?

The first question implies a structural use of language, as described in Chapter 2, and sets the therapist on the quest for the meaning behind the client's story. It may not be immediately clear to the client that the therapist has taken a decision which will determine the nature and parameters of the ensuing conversation. The latter question invites a clear definition of the focal issue. It acknowledges the part the therapist plays in constructing the direction of the therapeutic conversation.

Can you tell me more about the problem? v. Are there any
occasions when the problem doesn't happen or is in some way
different?

The first question invites problem talk. The client would provide examples of the behaviour, thoughts and feelings which he, or someone else, regards as problematic. As the therapist listens, she would seek further elaboration of the problem by reflecting, questioning or summarising the narrative in order to formulate an understanding or identify a pattern. As she listens to the content of the narrative, she will also attend to the verbal and non-verbal ways in which the client delivers it. The second question invites descriptions of those times when the problem is not happening. These are the exceptions when the client is somehow managing to control, manage or temporarily eliminate the problem. The therapist implies that the client is already engaging in solution behaviour. According to the solution-focused therapist, it is in these exceptional, non-problematic times that the seeds of the solution lie and it is about these that she will be most curious. Not surprisingly, people tend to talk about solutions in quite a different way to how they talk about their problems. Most people like to talk about successes and actually enjoy receiving credit for what they have achieved. One client who was virtually mute for months suddenly became quite eloquent when she changed from problem talk to solution talk.

How are we to understand the problem in the light of the
past? v. What will the future look like without the problem?

The former implies that the 'truth' about the problem lies in understanding the past and that the solution to the problem is intrinsically connected with the past and present experience of the client. It also focuses attention on finding causes to explain current behaviour. Many clients have come to believe, as a result of popular conceptions of therapy, that the primary purpose of therapy is to identify the roots of behaviour in one's personal or family history and that this may well prove to be a painful experience. Anticipation that this is the norm deters many people from going anywhere near a therapist.

The second question focuses attention on the client's picture of the future. This glimpse into the future is a powerful factor in explaining the client's current behaviour and also suggests the direction in which he hopes therapy might take him.

What defence mechanisms are operating? v. What can we utilise?

The first question reflects the therapist's analysis of the client's behaviour, in and out of sessions, as possibly being an unconscious strategy to defend a threatened ego. It introduces the idea of resistance, a concept which the solution-focused therapist disowns. The latter tends to see 'resistance' as being mutually constructed by both the therapist and the client, and that the withdrawal of co-operation by the client may indicate the need for the therapist to modify her approach. The second question attends to those qualities or strengths which the client possesses which could contribute to solving the problem. The solution-focused model is based on a fundamental belief in the essential competency of the client and always seeks to build on who the client is, rather than on what the therapist thinks he ought, or she would like him, to be.

What is the nature of the transference? v. How can the therapist collaborate with the client?

The psychodynamic approach attributes great significance to the transference and counter-transference in the therapeutic relationship, in the belief that they contain the vital information which will yield insights for the client. The present relationship echoes past relationships. The person-centred approach stresses the fundamental importance of the core conditions of the relationship, namely unconditional positive regard, congruence and empathy. The degree to which the therapist can offer this special relationship determines how much the client will be able to change. The relationship is the therapy. The second question also recognises the importance of the therapist–client relationship, but implies that it is the responsibility of the therapist to find ways of fostering the collaboration of the client. In SFT there is an assumption that the client can teach the therapist (who occupies a non-expert position) how to join with him effectively.

How many sessions? v. Have we achieved enough to end?

In some models of therapy it is the therapist who unilaterally decides the length of the course of treatment. An initial contract will stipulate a specific number of sessions with a review after, for example, six sessions. SFT does not employ this type of contract. The therapist may consult the client to find out how many sessions she thinks they may need, or may raise the possibility that one session might be sufficient. When therapy continues beyond the first session, the therapist and client will continually monitor progress in order to decide whether therapy should end.

Contracting and assessment

Contracting

The aim of the contract made between the therapist and the client is to establish a clear and agreed basis for the work. Clients approach therapists with a wide range of expectations as to what might happen and what their respective roles might be. Their own and other people's experience of seeking help; the degree to which they are coming of their own free will; their level of distress; and their perceptions of social attitudes towards their problem will all shape their expectations and how wary or suspicious they may be. In each case the therapist needs to find out what the client wants and whether therapy is the right form of help.

It is crucially important to listen carefully to the client's initial presentation as he will be acutely sensitive to the first response the therapist makes. If he does not feel heard he is likely to find ways of convincing the therapist how serious his problem is, such as withdrawing co-operation, sabotaging attempts at solution talk or leaving therapy.

In the early stages of contracting it is important to move at the client's pace. Brief does not mean rushed; pressurising the client is counterproductive and disrespectful. The solution-focused therapist aims to develop a co-operative 'joining' with the client in a warm, positive, accepting relationship which includes the adoption of a 'one down' (i.e. non-expert) position in which the client teaches the therapist about his view of the world and how the therapist could co-operate with him. This consultation is congruent with the rise of a consumer culture which wants its preferences and priorities to be taken seriously by providers. It echoes the supermarket campaign which asked its customers what it should *sell* rather than telling them what they should *buy*. Joining with the client involves a matching of the client's language, the offering of genuine compliments and a willingness to adapt therapeutic style in the light of what the client says is helpful or unhelpful. The therapist treats the client as the expert in his own life, while the therapist owns expertise in creating a therapeutic environment. The structure of the therapy depends upon a number of factors:

1   Agency policy which dictates the maximum number of sessions, length and possibly frequency.
2   The terms of specific contracts which demand that the client be seen quickly.
3   The attitude of the therapist towards brief therapy and its effectiveness. It is crucial that the therapist believes in what she is doing. If she regards brief therapy as second best and unlikely to produce lasting change, then she will fail to communicate the expectancy required for its effectiveness.

Most solution-focused therapists who are free to do so avoid contracting to see clients for a set number of sessions in the belief that it is possible to slow down the client's rate of progress by prescribing in advance the number of sessions required. The client might feel after one or two sessions that sufficient change has taken place. Committing both parties to six or more sessions, for example, runs the risk of the work expanding to fill the time available and thus losing its momentum and focus. It is more common practice to ask the client at the end of the first session whether he felt it had been helpful to talk and whether he would like to meet the therapist again, and if so when. Encouraging the client to take time to think about this helps to ensure that the client retains choice and power over his therapy. This devolving of power to the client might not suit everyone. Some might feel more secure and confident in feeling that the therapist knows how many sessions are necessary and that they can plan their lives more easily around a structured course. One of the possible disadvantages for the client in not being contracted to a specific number of sessions might be that he feels uncertain about raising issues because he does not know whether there is sufficient time to deal with them properly. Clients sometimes need reassuring that they have a right to the time they need and that they are not wasting the therapist's time.

The frequency of meetings is also a subject of negotiation, there being no set rule about weekly meetings. The therapist tries to fit in as far as possible with the pattern which most suits the individual client. Imposing a schedule upon clients increases the risk that they will drop out prematurely. In addition to the fact that weekly attendance can pose serious practical problems for many clients, a longer interval between sessions can provide them with more opportunities to develop their problem-solving strategies. However, setting intervals too far apart can destroy the focused intensity and momentum needed. Some models of brief therapy advocate that the client keeps a session or a number of sessions 'in the bank' to be drawn upon, either after a stipulated period of time or when a difficulty arises. Another option is to hold weekly sessions for the first two or three weeks in order to build a sense of momentum, and to meet at fortnightly or monthly intervals thereafter. Clients have different attitudes towards the amount of time they are able or willing to devote to resolving their problems. This ranges from a wish for a 'fast fix', to a belief that only long-term work will be effective.

With respect to the length of sessions, there is nothing sacrosanct about the fifty-minute hour. Concentrating for that length of time is difficult for many people, including tired therapists. There are situations which demand that amount of time and more, but there are also many other occasions when it would be more therapeutic to end the session earlier – for example, when the client has made a decision or come to a point of resolution. It can be more beneficial to end on a strong, positive note than to prolong the session unduly.

Assessment
Some SFT practitioners do not screen clients for suitability but prefer to work with whoever comes or is sent to them. Their rationale is that there are no clear predictive signs to indicate or contra-indicate a particular client's ability to engage in and gain from SFT. In SFT there is no clear distinction between assessment and therapy. Therapy starts even before the therapist meets the client. Some forms of assessment run counter to the spirit and constructionist philosophy of SFT in that they emphasise deficits, pathology, crises, failure and trauma. There is insufficient recognition of the coping strategies, the strength of character, the courage and the stamina which the client has needed to cope to date. Recurring detailed assessments of this kind can disempower the client and are anti-therapeutic. In the initial stages of an SFT first session the therapist seeks to discover what the client

perceived as helpful or unhelpful in previous therapy relationships. This provides the therapist with important information on
how to join with the client and foster co-operation.

Visitor, complainant and customer

De Shazer (1988) uses the terms visitor, complainant and
customer to distinguish between clients with different agendas.
From a constructionist point of view, the description belongs not
so much to the client as to the constructed relationship between
the two parties. A visiting relationship is one in which the client
does not think he has a problem or does not want to be in
therapy or both. A complainant one is where the person is
willing to discuss the problem but sees the solution as lying
elsewhere. A customer relationship is where the client recognises
that he has a particular problem and wants to do something
about it. It would be a mistake to treat these three 'types' of
relationship in the same way. On occasions, the visiting or complainant relationship can become a customer one when the two
parties manage to negotiate a clear benefit which the client could
gain from therapy. On other occasions a negotiated referral or an
agreement to discontinue counselling might be the outcome.
Fisch, Weakland and Segal (1982: 39) use the analogy of the
window-shopper who slips into a shop to keep out of a heavy
shower, and who has no intention of buying anything but may
try to look as if she has, to describe the ambivalence many clients
bring to the first session.

Figure 3.3 represents various positions clients might adopt
with respect to change. These positions may reflect a lack of
knowledge, awareness, motivation or the social skills to move the
problem forward. The therapist needs to meet the client where he
is at the moment he comes into therapy.

The ideal solution-focused client might present for therapy and
say: 'I am very clear what I would like to change in my life and I
am willing to invest a lot of effort into making those changes. I
have already begun to make progress and I would like to build
on my strengths to develop those solutions. I will be clear and
specific in describing what is happening in the area of my life
which is causing me concern. I do not wish to explore my
life story or search for hidden meanings to my life. I want to co-
operate with you and put into effect any ideas we may generate

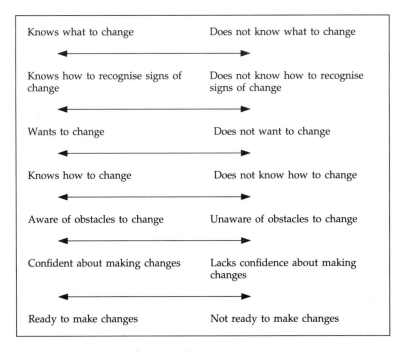

Figure 3.3   *Spectrum of change–client positions*

about change. I will report back to you promptly on my progress. I will want to end therapy as soon as I have begun to make progress.' It is likely that clients who are motivated to change will share some of these sentiments. In pre-session literature clients should be informed about the type of therapy on offer so that they can make an informed choice about whether or not to participate.

Focal issue

Most forms of brief therapy stress the importance of having a focal or central issue for the work. The clearer and more specific the agenda, the greater the likelihood that the therapy will be purposeful and effective. In SFT the focus of the work is the problem presented by the client. Barret-Kruse (1994) describes the presenting problem as 'a gift to the therapist'. The framing of the problem and the solution are matters for negotiation. This can present particular challenges in cases where the safety of another person is involved. Yet even in abuse investigations, it may be possible for the worker and the client to form a collaborative solution-focused relationship. The closer the therapist can keep to the client's agenda, the more likely the client will feel motivated to change. By tracking the client's agenda the therapist develops an empathic and collaborative relationship. The agenda has to be specific, clear and concrete in its formulation, with minimal opportunities for expansion. It is not always possible to achieve this in a first session, as clients are often confused, anxious, overwhelmed and unsure how therapy can help them.

Solution-focused therapists report that many clients find it easier to engage in conversation about solutions than they do about the problem. In SFT the therapist accepts what the client brings and does not speculate about underlying issues or the origins of the problem. The priority is to find a common language to describe what the client wants to change and to begin to explore how those changes would affect the client's life. This is not easy; as various studies have shown, the client's experience of therapy is more complex than the therapist imagines (Metcalf and Thomas 1994).

Clients often present with multiple interlocking problems which require prioritising, not in the sense that once one problem is 'solved', attention then turns to the next on the list, but in the sense that the client agrees that a single issue will be the focus of the work and that other problems will only be discussed in so far as they affect the central issue. The therapist needs to find leverage, namely a solvable problem which the client wants and is able to work upon.

EXAMPLE

> *Therapist*: So you would like to talk about the way you and your partner cannot agree about controlling your children. You have mentioned that there are other problems about work and health, but am I right that you want to concentrate on the disagreements with your partner and that the other matters will only come up if they throw light upon that?

This agreement allows the client to introduce relevant material from other problem areas, but only in so far as it sheds light on the central issue. It also gives the therapist permission to keep the client to the point. Steenbarger (1994) concluded from his review of various studies, that brief therapy is most suitable for clients who are highly aware of focal problem patterns and are able to form a working alliance. Clients who present with broad, diffuse and poorly understood patterns and who need considerable time to form a trusting alliance are more likely to need an extended period of exploratory work. In my experience, it is a great advantage when clients can articulate their problem and their goals, but it does not mean that initial vagueness and lack of clarity about the future disqualifies them from brief solution-focused work. It simply means that the therapist has to work harder and take longer.

Principles

There are a number of principles or assumptions which guide solution-focused work. They apply both to how the client should approach the problem and to how the therapist should conduct the therapy.

If it isn't broken don't fix it

SFT is a competency-based approach. It emphasises that people *have* problems, rather than that they *are* problems; or, to be more precise, problems happen in the relationship between the person and the social environment, they do not belong to the person as if she lived in a vacuum. SFT does not see clients as being sick (and therefore in need of a cure) or damaged (and therefore in need of repair), but as temporarily unable to overcome a life difficulty because they have not yet found a way out of or round it. Instead of focusing on pathology (the answer doesn't lie there), it seeks out and builds upon what is healthy and functioning in people's lives. We can only build upon strengths.

SFT encourages a period of problem-free talk with the client (George, Iveson and Ratner 1990). This may take the form of a preliminary informal conversation (not to be confused with small talk) about what the client enjoys doing at times when the problem is not affecting him. This can often provide useful clues to the therapist when she comes to look for client strengths and to devise strategies. The therapist may disclose information about herself or the therapy which she feels would help this particular client.

Building on what is right, rather than fixing what is wrong (O'Hanlon and Weiner-Davis 1989) also helps to limit the agenda and to keep therapy brief. When clients feel overwhelmed by a problem, they tend to lose sight of their strengths and resources. Skott-Myhre (1992) outlines the basic principles of a competency-based approach as being:

- What people do is based upon what they believe to be true about the world.

The first task of the therapist is to hear and validate the client's experience and subjective perception of the world. This subjective view may not be consistent with the 'facts' (the historical truth) but it is the client's 'truth'.

- What people believe to be true is shaped and developed through the conversations they have with each other.

People do not acquire their experience in a vacuum, but rather in a social context in which language describes that experience to other people. We need to know the audience for the conversation in which people engage.

- Each person is embedded in a unique dialogic ecology.

There is a mutual dialogue between the individual, other people and the social and cultural environment in which he lives. A useful tool for understanding the social context of this dialogue, based on constructionist epistemology, is discourse analysis (Widdicombe 1993). It sets out to understand the rules which govern social intercourse, and assumes that people use language to construct the world according to their own interests, rather than as a representation of an objective reality out there. It is not possible for anyone to approach the discourse of another from a position of neutrality since we all have our own filters through which we interpret the world. The issue of power is closely allied to the dominance of some forms of discourse over others – for example, white and male over black and female.

- The nature and substance of this ecology is constantly changing.

Discourse analysis contends that meanings are multiple and constantly shifting according to the audience. The language of the word games used in therapy is itself in a state of flux. It could be argued that the dominant form of therapeutic discourse to date, psychoanalysis, is giving way to more pragmatic models which do not carry the weight of ideological baggage which the former collected.

- Each and every person is inherently competent and has all the resources necessary for change.
- The role of therapy is not to create change but to discover where change is occurring and amplify it.

This is a key strategy in SFT – building on what the client brings and on what is already making a difference to the problem.

- Therapy need not take a long time.

This belief attacks the notion that effective therapy needs to be long term. But this does not mean that brief therapy is the right choice for every client. Some clients require long-term therapy and to offer anything less would be to cheat them of what they need.

Small change can lead to bigger changes
One of the characteristics of solution-focused work is the way in which it breaks down the process of change into small manageable steps. According to Rosenbaum, Hoyt and Talmon (1990) there are three advantages to such an approach:

1   It takes the pressure off both therapist and client, so that neither tries too hard. Trying too hard to bring about change can itself cause problems. There are times when it is wiser to do less rather than more.
2   The client is more likely to be willing to make a small change than a big one. There are always exceptions to this of course and the therapist needs to respond to the client who is ready for rapid and radical change.
3   Any kind of movement may suffice to ignite hope in the client. Generating hope and confidence, providing it is not false, is an important ingredient in brief therapy. Clients, feeling overwhelmed by their problems and ambivalent about change, often find making any kind of start a daunting prospect. The SFT approach is to find a small, but significant,

starting point for initiating change. As someone once said, 'if you think you're too small to be effective, you've never been in bed with a mosquito!'

EXAMPLE

Frances feels that there is virtually no constructive communication with her partner. The starting point for change may be a particular time and event, such as the sequence of events which takes place when one partner returns home. The client may be asked: Who greets whom, when, how? What would happen if it were handled differently? If he felt welcomed home, how would that make a difference? What would you do if you were to welcome him home in a different way? What would need to happen for that to happen? Could you do that?

We are changing all of the time, only the pace and direction is uncertain. The skilled therapist respects and matches the client's pace, neither holding her back, nor pressurising her to move more quickly than she wants or feels able. At times, the pace is slow and measured, at others fast and radical. Initiating change can often have repercussions beyond the focal starting point. Experiencing change can restore the person's sense of choice and control and encourage the making of further changes.

However, changing one element in the system, however small, does not guarantee that the consequences will be wholly helpful or constructive, at least in the short term. Changing behaviour or attitudes can bring negative effects as well, such as further oppression, punishment, sanctions, a heightened sense of how much still needs to be done, or an increased sense of inadequacy. Initiating change can trigger memories of past hurts, regrets, failures or losses.

If it's working keep doing it

The therapist encourages the client to keep doing what she has shown she can already do. This constructive behaviour may have started prior to the therapy (pre-session change). Clients may need to sustain the new pattern of behaviour for some time before they feel confident about maintaining it. At first this new way of handling the problem may feel artificial and make them feel self-conscious. They would prefer it to feel more natural and real. However, experimenting with new behaviour is like learning your lines in a play or the notes in your music before you can really get into the part or become musical. Therapy can provide opportunities for rehearsal and experimentation.

If it's not working stop doing it
In keeping with the MRI principle of abandoning failed solutions, the solution-focused therapist encourages clients to do something different (almost anything) to break the failure cycle. This may run counter to family scripts (for the therapist and the client), such as 'if at first you don't succeed, try, try again'. It can often happen that changing the time and place in which the client 'does' the problem can break the 'stuck' routine.

Keep therapy as simple as possible
There is a danger that the ideology of the therapist, particularly if it entails looking for hidden explanations and unconscious factors, will complicate the relationship. Solution-focused therapists advocate minimal intrusion into the client's life and look for ways of ending the relationship as soon as possible. The constructionist position dispenses with the notion that the therapist has, through her training, a privileged view of the client's problem.

Process model of solution-focused therapy

Figure 3.4 describes three main themes which emerge in solution-focused conversations and the interventions which take place under them. As with all such models, it attempts to map out the territory, it is not the territory itself. The process is not a logical linear sequence of events. There is a flexibility which enables the therapist to respond to the individual client by weaving the dialogue between problem/solution; past/future; individual/system; goal/strategies. Although there are standard formulas, such as the miracle question and the first session task, the process as a whole is not mechanical. There are three types of discourse which take place.

- Change discourse is a therapeutic conversation which emphasises the changing experience of the client in relation to his or her ability to solve the problem.
- Solution discourse comprises the intermediate interventions used by the therapist to help the client bridge the gap

Change discourse	Solution discourse	Strategy discourse
problem deconstruction	acknowledge/validate problem	define solvable central problem/focus
seek competence	compliment and affirm	utilise/reinforce learning
seek exceptions	miracle question	clarify goals/identify existing and transferable solutions
set goals	scale goals	establish endings and evaluate
circular questions	identify and reframe interactional patterns	plan new interactional patterns
behavioural language	clear specific observable descriptions	deliver message give task

Therapist help is characterised by: optimism hope support confidence collaboration empathy competence

Figure 3.4   *Solution-focused process model*

between the current change processes and the strategies required to obtain the goals of the client.

• Strategy discourse is a co-operative engagement between the therapist and the client to design and monitor the implementation of realistic plans towards the achievement of the client's goals.

Change discourse
From the very beginning of the relationship, the therapist focuses on the theme of change. She communicates a belief that change is already taking place and that she expects change to continue to take place. In SFT, this climate of change encompasses the time prior to the first session. The person with whom the client makes the appointment asks the client to notice whether any changes take place between the time of making the appointment and the first session (known as pre-session change). Typically, the therapist will inquire about these changes early on in the first session.

In the ebb and flow of change discourse, the therapist paces and times the questions which form the main speech events of the discourse. Questions open therapeutic space and offer new or different ways of thinking about situations. The therapist is curious about what is already happening in the client's life. The client becomes recruited into change-oriented language. Depending on the ability of the client to engage in this way, the therapist either continues to develop the change theme, or allows the client to engage in further descriptions of the problem.

The task of the therapist is to find leverage for change. The prospect of change often creates ambivalence in the client, with discourse about change typically swinging between problem and change talk, and between conversation about the past, the present and the future. If the therapist unsuccessfully attempts to initiate change talk, then it is necessary to return to problem exploration until another shift becomes possible. It can happen that a client is unable to engage in change talk in any meaningful or sustained way for some time and in some cases never manages to do so. It is with such clients that a solution-focused method fails.

The principal elements in the discourse on change are:

1 *Competence talk* The therapist identifies and affirms strengths and qualities of the client which can be utilised in solving the problem (de Shazer 1988). The coping mechanisms which have been used by the client to date are acknowledged and reinforced.

2 *Exception talk* Freedman and Combs (1993: 296) describe seeking exceptions as: 'ways in which people recover experiences at odds with their dominant story. By highlighting different events, they are opening space for the authoring of new stories.' The therapist attempts to engage the client in seeking exceptions to the problem, i.e. those occasions when the problem is not happening or is being managed better. This includes the search for transferable solutions (Berg 1991, de Shazer 1994). It is also helpful to identify 'solutions' which have worked or indeed failed in the past.

3 *Context-changing talk* The therapist helps to put the problem into a different frame, one which will make it more solvable (O'Hanlon and Wilk 1987). The frame used in SFT is interactional, i.e. it recognises that the way people behave and the problems they have develop within the context of the people and the situations which surround them. The level of focus is

on the observable patterns of behaviour. Change comes from redefining the situation or altering the problem patterns. Circular statements or questions are used to explore the client's network.

4   *Deconstructing the problem*   The discourse about change employs descriptive language. It uses the client's words to clarify the changes which are the client's goals. It avoids abstract words, such as depression, self-esteem and stress, in favour of a detailed description of the client's ordinary day-to-day behaviour. The therapist often, but not always, translates the client's feelings, attitudes or personality characteristics into observable behaviour. There is an assumption that inner thoughts and feelings usually manifest themselves in behaviour.

Solution discourse

The discourse on solutions need not succeed that on change in terms of time, but may occur simultaneously with it. The principal elements of this discourse are:

1   *Formation of a collaborative relationship*   Rapport can emerge when the client begins to sense that the therapist and he are working together and making a difference to the problem. Empathy need not be a precondition for client change, but can accompany or follow it. It is sometimes achieved as a consequence of the client attributing positive change to the helpfulness of the therapist. This collaborative stance is oriented towards client goals rather than to the investigation and understanding of the problem. It consists of support, encouragement, compliments, affirmation, attention to the client's goals and active participation on the part of the therapist. There is a commitment to respecting what the client wants, providing it is not unlawful or unethical. Once the therapist has adequately understood the client's difficulties and the client feels accepted, both parties co-create an agenda for change.

2   *The miracle question*   This is a key intervention typically used in a first session, but which may also reappear in subsequent sessions. It aims to identify existing solutions and resources and to clarify the client's goals in realistic terms. It is a future-oriented question designed to help the client describe, as

clearly and as specifically as possible, what his life will be like once the problem is solved or is being managed better.

3   *Scaling*   The primary purpose of scaling is to set client goals, measure progress and establish priorities for action. Scaling questions are also used to discover how motivated the client is towards change and how confident he is about solving the problem.

4   *Reframing*   By reframing, the therapist helps the client to find another way of looking at the problem, one which will hopefully increase the chances of the client overcoming the problem. In SFT the meaning of the client's experiences is negotiable, depending on the outcome of the linguistic trans-actions in which the client and therapist engage. The purpose of the therapeutic dialogue is to negotiate jointly a meaning to the client's situation which will create the possibility of change for him.

Strategy discourse

This consists partly of identifying existing, but until now, devalued strategies in the client's life. Again, timing and sensi-tivity are crucial in sensing the optimum moment for engaging the client in a discourse about strategy. The interruption of old patterns, even if they were clearly failing, and the adoption of new patterns, raises fears, doubts and anxieties in most clients. The issue of ownership of strategies is clearly important. The main elements in the discourse on strategy are:

1   *Utilisation*   This is the mobilisation by the therapist of the client's experiences, values, skills, ideas and feelings in pursuit of the client's desired goal. The confidence and moti-vation of the client will obviously be important factors in the choice of strategies. The therapist recognises and reinforces the client's prior learning.

2   *Development of solutions*   The solution-focused method advo-cates incremental changes, small advances towards the goal, with the emphasis being on the client continuing to do what is already proving to be helpful. These steps emerge from discovering exceptions to the problem and from answers to the 'miracle question'. They include the abandonment of 'solutions' which have repeatedly failed in the past.

3   *Clarifications of endings and evaluation*   The client's goals are the sought-after outcomes of the therapy. The therapist explores with the client how these can be achieved and in which order of priority. During and after each session, the therapist evaluates with the client whether what they are doing together is proving helpful.

4   *The message and task giving*   This is the concluding stage in each session. The therapist summarises the constructive strategies described by the client in the session and reinforces and compliments progress. In most cases she will give the client a specific task to carry out before the next session.

4

The First Session

Therapy is often a matter of tipping the first domino.

Milton Erickson, cited in Rossi (1980)

Aims of the first session

In the first session the solution-focused therapist seeks:

- To form a collaborative relationship with the client.
- To create a climate for change.
- To clarify as far as possible the goals of therapy.
- To discover the client's resources.
- To explore tasks.

It is important for the reader to bear in mind that written accounts of therapy fail to capture the intangibles in the therapeutic relationship. There is a danger of giving the impression that solution-focused therapy (SFT) is a slick and mechanical operation devoid of mystery. It needs to be reiterated that how we relate to clients as human beings is more significant than any techniques or theories. Technique is no substitute for a relationship built on respectful and attentive listening, reflective silences, empathy, genuineness, immediacy and acceptance.

Forming a collaborative relationship

Prior to coming for therapy, a client might hold views which make the beginning of the relationship difficult. They may:

1 Have previous negative experience of seeking help. This can be turned into a resource if the therapist is able and willing to explore what was or was not useful on those occasions. There

is little point in repeating the mistakes of previous therapists and there is every point in finding out what the client found useful or thought would have been useful.

2   Have fixed ideas about what should happen in therapy. Clients who have been to other therapists or read popular psychology self-help books are likely to hold views as to what the role of both parties should be. It can come as something of a surprise for them to encounter a therapist who shows little interest in case history or problem behaviour, particularly if they thought that such an investigation was essential for therapy to take place.

In SFT, the therapist first listens attentively to the client's concerns. The SFT literature's rare mention of empathy reflects an absence of discussion to date about the therapeutic relationship itself and the person of the therapist in particular. De Shazer (1996) states that he assumes empathy when working with clients, but is reluctant to use the word or define it. O'Hanlon and Beadle (1994) do not use the term, preferring to talk about validating and acknowledging the client's experience. The notion of empathy itself is not however as simple as first appears. Bachelor (1988) in a study of empathy found that 44 per cent of clients perceived their therapist's empathy to be cognitive in nature, 30 per cent as affective, 18 per cent as sharing and 7 per cent as nurturant. She concluded that empathy had different meanings for different clients and that therapists should not consider it to be a universal construct. Duncan (1992: 21) described empathy as:

> therapist attitudes and behaviours that place the client's perceptions and experiences above theoretical content and personal values; empathy is operationalised by therapist attempts not only to accept the internal frame of reference of the client, but more importantly to work within the expressed meaning system of the client.

This is very similar to de Shazer's (1994) term 'reader-focused', which he uses to describe a person-centred approach to the client's narrative, in contrast to a 'text-focused' approach.

The solution-focused therapist uses empathy to form a therapeutic alliance, although he is unlikely to reflect feelings back as often as in a person-centred approach. His aim is to develop a respectful collaborative stance which is oriented towards client goals. There is an implication in SFT that empathic rapport emerges as the client begins to sense that the therapist and she are working together in making a difference to the problem. From this perspective, empathy need not be a precondition for client change, but can accompany or follow it. It is sometimes achieved as a consequence of the client attributing positive change to the helpfulness of the therapist. Empathy is characterised by support, encouragement, compliments, affirmation and close attention to the client's goals. Respecting what the client wants is the core value, providing it is not unlawful or unethical. Once the client's difficulties have been adequately understood and the client feels accepted, both parties can co-create an agenda for change.

Creating a climate for change

Clients who feel unsure about therapy may need to be reassured that they don't have to change, but that they need to do different things or stop doing certain things in order to meet their goals. From a constructionist viewpoint there are no 'things' to be changed, such as one's personality, but there are choices to be made in one's interactions. Since the current 'problematic' situation is one the client does not want, she needs to renegotiate the problem or alter the behaviour which she, or someone else, defines as problematic. In the first place, the therapist sets out to engage the client in a therapeutic conversation concerning the client's changing experience in relation to the problem. This differs from the exploratory stage in other therapies, the purpose of which is principally to gather information from the client in order to understand the problem better. In the SFT approach the therapist pays particular attention to strengths, skills and coping strategies which the client is already using.

Pre-session change
From the very beginning the therapist focuses on the theme of change. The therapist communicates a belief that change is already taking place and that he expects change to continue. In SFT, this climate of change encompasses time even prior to the client meeting with the therapist. When making an appointment, the client is asked to notice whether any changes take place between the time of making the appointment and the first session (pre-session change). Typically, the therapist will inquire about

these changes early on in the first session. In the past, therapists often ignored or even denied that clients had begun to solve their problems before they engaged in therapy. Some practitioners dismissed reported change as illusory, temporary or as denial and a flight into health in order to avoid facing the real problems. Weiner-Davis, de Shazer and Gingerich (1987) explored the changes which take place in the client's life in the interval between making an appointment and coming to see the therapist. They reported that of thirty parents with family problems, twenty (66 per cent) reported having observed positive pre-session changes. They were asked three questions:

1   Many times people notice in between the time they make the appointment for therapy and the first session that things already seem different. What have you noticed about your situation?

If the client was able to answer the first question the parent was then asked the next two questions:

2   Do these changes relate to the reason why you came for therapy?
3   Are these the kinds of changes you would like to continue to have happen?

They state that in addition to the twenty who reported positive changes, the remainder often recalled pre-treatment changes later in the session. Lawson (1994), in replicating this research, interviewed eighty-two clients. Of the eighty-two, fifty-one (62 per cent) reported having observed positive pre-session change, whereas the remaining thirty-one (37.8 per cent) reported either no change (twenty-eight), or reported that things seemed worse (three). Of the fifty-one reporting positive pre-session change, forty-nine reported yes to question 2 (changes are related to the reason they came for therapy) and question 3 (these were the kinds of changes they wanted to continue to happen). Thus 59.75 per cent (forty-nine) of the respondents reported that positive change was occurring with regard to their presenting problem.

Positive pre-session change is empowering for the client because the changes have taken place independently of the therapist and, therefore, the credit belongs solely to the client. By granting recognition to pre-session change, the therapist can build on what the client has already begun. The client may present the therapist with clear clues about strategies, beliefs, values and skills which are transferable into solution construction. This 'flying start' helps to accelerate the process of change and increases the likelihood of the therapy being brief.

Clients are often pleasantly surprised when the therapist acknowledges the efforts and progress they have made. They may have come into therapy feeling embarrassed, a failure or ashamed. They may expect criticism, blame or even a feeling of humiliation. Instead they experience respect for their struggle to date and a genuine celebration of their achievements. This can be an emotional experience for some clients. Feeling that the therapist understands, helps to lower their defences. It injects a note of hope, that things are beginning to move in the right direction and that perhaps they have done the hardest part already. Sometimes coming to see the therapist is the hardest part! This can be particularly true if the therapist is of a different gender or race from the client.

> *Therapist*: Have you noticed any differences since you contacted us last week?
> *Client*: When I phoned you I was rock bottom. I just couldn't stop crying. I couldn't eat, sleep or go out. I still feel pretty awful but I'm not crying so much.
> *Therapist*: So what helped?
> *Client*: My friends have been very supportive. They have made sure I've not been on my own.
> *Therapist*: So it's felt better having someone with you most of the time.
> *Client*: I don't know what I would have done without them.
> *Therapist*: Has anything else helped?
> *Client*: I told myself life had to go on. There's nothing I can do about it.
> *Therapist*: You feel you have to make the best of it and somehow get on with things.
> *Client*: I know it's going to take time to get used to it.
> *Therapist*: Has anything else helped?
> *Client*: For the first couple of days I drank quite a lot and I felt terrible when I woke up in the morning.
> *Therapist*: So you've found that drinking too much isn't going to help you much.

Clients may not initially see differences in the situation as being significant. They may dismiss them as marginal, accidental or due to unusual circumstances. As in other parts of the model, it is imperative that the therapist is not deflected by such answers. Clients who initially state that they don't know how things happened, often volunteer an explanation later, once they have had time to think things over. The therapist's curiosity and belief that the changes did not happen by accident, or his surprise that the problem is apparently the same as last week, can prompt the client to recall incidents which cast more light on what is happening. An intriguing study by McKeel and Weiner-Davis (1995) found that when clients were asked the pre-session change question in a way which implied that their situations had *not* changed since they made the appointment, 67 per cent reported their situation was the same. It would appear that if the therapist does not believe in pre-session change, then neither does the client!

In examining the ebb and flow of change, the therapist paces and times the questions which form the main interventions. Questions are used to open therapeutic space and offer the client new or different ways of thinking about situations. The therapist is curious about what is already happening or could happen in the client's life. The client becomes recruited into using change-oriented language. Depending on the ability of the client to engage in this way, the therapist either continues to develop the theme of change, or allows the client to give a further account of the problem. Typical questions used at this stage include:

- What is happening at the moment which makes you more hopeful that you can change the situation?
- In what ways is today a good time to start to sort things out?
- What is different about your situation now that made you decide it was time to come for help and try to sort things out?
- What have you come here today to change?

Most solution-focused therapists agree that it is necessary, and clients expect, that there will be sufficient opportunity for them to tell their story and to feel accepted by the therapist. Having a clearly identified problem may in itself help the client by relieving his anxiety and establishing his credibility. It may also be important to 'label' the problem in order to gain resources for its treatment. It is essential in a multicultural society to recognise and respect that there are many different philosophies about life, suffering and evil. A fatalistic view of life, for example, may be a cultural value which enables a person to accommodate change, develop coping mechanisms and build character. Without such an experience of being heard, believed and respected, the client is likely to be reluctant to explore the possibility of change. Nylund and Corsiglia (1994) criticise a misuse of SFT which pressurises clients to discuss change before they are ready. They describe this as solution 'forced' therapy and suggest that it is likely to leave clients frustrated and angry.

The task of the therapist in an SFT first session, following the validation of the client's problem, is to negotiate a language with the client which allows for the possibility of change. Thinking about and constructing change may create ambivalence in people (they fear that change might make the problem worse in some way). Consequently, discussion of change swings between problem and change talk, with the focus moving between the past, the present and the future. It is important to note that what is happening in the encounter is that the two people are pooling their linguistic resources to devise a narrative which allows for the client doing something different from what he has done up till now. The client may be relieved to know that he does not need to change but that something he is doing or not doing needs to change. If the therapist fails to initiate or sustain change talk, then it is usually necessary to return to exploration of the problem until a linguistic shift becomes possible. Sometimes a client cannot or will not engage in change talk for some time and in some cases never manages to do so. It is with such clients that a solution-focused method fails and some other approach is required. Other clients feel stretched and excited by talking about the future, having feared that the therapist would insist that they rake over their past in great detail despite their own feelings that this would not be helpful. Talking about the future often helps to move the defences which the client had in place.

The therapist models the use of descriptive language in exploring the changes in the client's life. He uses the client's own words to clarify the observable changes which are necessary to reach the client's goals. He avoids abstract and vague words, such as depression, low self-esteem, attention-seeking and stress, in favour of concrete descriptions of the client's ordinary day-to-day behaviour. The therapist often translates the client's conversation about feelings or attitudes or personality characteristics into examples of observable behaviour. This emphasis on external behaviour does not, however, exclude conversation about feelings and attitudes.

> *Therapist*: So what are the signs for you that you're feeling depressed?
> *Client*: I stay in bed most of the day. I don't care about how I look. I hardly ever go out unless I absolutely have to. The others have to look after themselves, I can't even be bothered eating.
> *Therapist*: What else is happening when you feel depressed?
> *Client*: I avoid people as much as possible. I have no energy or enthusiasm for anything. I give up doing the things I like. I feel like I want to be left on my own.

This dialogue may not clarify why the client chose to name her problem as depression but her descriptive account is of behaviours which presumably she would like to change. Her clear pictorial language makes it easier for the therapist to understand her unique experience of depression and what she would like the goals of therapy to be – for example, to be able to get out of bed, to take care of her appearance, to go out of the house, to have more energy, to take an interest in people again.

Establishing the goals of therapy

> While we pursue the unattainable, we make impossible the realizable.
>
> Robert Ardrey (1970)

> What we call the beginning is often the end, and to make an end is to make a beginning. The end is where we start from.
>
> T.S. Eliot (1963) *The Four Quartets*

It is the task of the therapist to help the client define her problem in a solvable way and to generate clear, simple, attainable goals for therapy. The client goals may not always be reconcilable with the goals of the referrer and that is another challenge for the therapist. Goals are the incentives, the motivators for change, which will sustain the client to persist in making changes which in the short term may be painful, but in the long term will bring the desired benefits the client is seeking. In McDonald's (1994) study of SFT there was a significant correlation between positive outcome and the successful negotiation of specific goals for treatment. The outcome was less successful when goals were defined negatively and least successful when the goals were non-specific. In SFT the therapist attempts to clarify with clients what they hope will be happening should therapy be successful. This is not always possible as clients can not only be vague and puzzled about their problems, but also equally vague as to what would constitute a good outcome. Therapy is ineffectual when both parties feel unsure or at cross purposes about the goal of the work. They may not know what they are trying to achieve and have little idea as to whether or not they are heading in the right direction. As a result, therapy can drift and become unfocused and unproductively lengthy. In order to avoid this, the therapist tries to negotiate with the client a clear ending to the therapy:

- If therapy were to prove really worth while for you, what would be happening that is not happening for you at the moment? What would have stopped happening?
- What will be the first signs for you that you don't need to continue with therapy?

Sometimes it is possible to find out how long the client thinks it is going to take before things start to get better. The therapist may ask a time-projected question, such as:

- If I were to meet you in three/six months time and you were telling me things were much better, not perfect but better than they are now, what would you tell me that you, or anyone else, did which was helpful?

The therapist is able to build on the answers to such questions in order to construct strategies and solutions. A client may under-standably want the therapist to take away her painful feelings of anxiety, fear, sadness or despair, but she may also need to accept that these 'bad' feelings could continue for some time and that they could be giving her important information on how she should act. Some clients are in seemingly inescapable situations in which they are unlikely to feel positive, for example, they are on sick leave due to stress following a traumatic incident; they may have to face internal inquiries or disciplinary procedures at some stage; there could be an impending inquest or court case; lengthy medical treatment; recurring publicity; a job change or loss. In some cases, the client may have to learn to come to terms with a situation (if only I could turn the clock back) which is not going to alter. In others, it is more likely that the client needs to change what he is doing before he will experience a change in feelings, although it is not easy to act constructively while feeling unsure, frightened or anxious. Some clients believe that they are unable to do anything until they feel better; others feel they are entitled to be happy all the time and will not settle for simply feeling happy more often than they do at the moment. Such rigid 'all or nothing' attitudes are not realistic and can helpfully be challenged. A similar difficulty arises with clients who want cast-iron guarantees that achieving their goals will bring the benefits for which they hope. Visions, unfortunately, can turn out to be mirages and dreams can become nightmares.

The solution-focused method usually aims for incremental changes; small advances towards client goals, with the emphasis on the client continuing to do what is already helpful. These steps are based on the exceptions to the problem and on answers to the miracle question.

The miracle question

> You must give birth to your images. They are the future waiting to be born . . . fear not the strangeness you feel. The future must enter into you long before it happens.

> Rainer Maria Rilke (1990: 115)

This is a key intervention typically used in a first session, but also in subsequent sessions. It aims to identify existing solutions and resources and to clarify the client's goals in realistic terms. It is a future-oriented question which seeks to help the client describe, as clearly and specifically as possible, what her life will be like once she solves the problem or manages it better.

The question, devised by Steve de Shazer (1988), follows a standard formula:

> Imagine when you go to sleep one night a miracle happens and the problems we've been talking about disappear. As you were asleep, you did not know that a miracle had happened. When you woke up what would be the first signs for you that a miracle had happened?

This question is similar to Adler's 'fundamental question' – 'what would be different if all your problems were solved?' (1925). It is also similar to Erickson's crystal ball technique, in which he invited clients to look into the future and then explain how what had happened had come about. He also used the technique of inviting clients to imagine a date on a calendar when things were better, then to work backwards to see what had happened at various points along the way. The miracle question should be asked slowly with pauses between the phrases to allow the client to enter into the spirit of the question. If it feels appropriate the therapist may invite the client to use her senses to imagine life without the problem – what would she see/taste/hear/touch/smell?

The miracle question can help the client to clarify goals and the means to achieve them. It can identify existing solutions and resources while creating a climate of change. Though it raises the possibility of life being different, it should not engender false hopes which may lead to disillusionment or even despair. The miracle question is not a fantasy journey after which the client will make miracles happen. The intention is to generate a rich, detailed practical description of life without the problem. How we picture the future determines how we act in the present.

The imaginary format gives the client permission to rise above negative, limited thinking and to develop a picture of the solution. It is a way of encouraging the client to escape temporarily from a preoccupation with problems, in order to divert energy into solution construction. Many clients feel stuck in the past and find it very difficult to think about or believe in the future. They feel fatalistic about the past, the present and the future and can only conceive of it as being more of what they have always had. Many people have very restricted choices and limited control of their destinies. The therapist needs to be aware of, and sensitive to, the contextual structures which shape the lives of their clients.

EXAMPLE

> *Therapist*: Let me ask you a strange question Anne, which many people find helpful.

This introduction warns the client that the next question is unusual, but suggests that trying to answer it will be worth the effort because other people have gained from it.

> *Therapist*: Imagine that when you go to sleep tonight a miracle happens and all of the difficulties which you have been having at home disappear. Because you are asleep, you don't know that a miracle has happened. When you wake up in the morning what will be the first signs for you that a miracle has happened?
> *Client*: I don't know [*Pause*] . . . we'd feel closer together . . .

A first response is often vague and general. The therapist needs to support the client in finding visible evidence that something has changed.

Therapist: So what would you be seeing if you were both feeling closer to each other?

Throughout the therapy, the therapist adopts the language used by the client.

Client: We'd feel relaxed and calm and just generally happier.

While validating the client's feelings, it is helpful to translate feelings into observable behaviour. Fisch (1994) offers a variation of the miracle question:

Assume you wake up tomorrow morning and, for some reason or another, the feeling you have is no longer a problem. What will be different then? How will you know?

As Quick (1994) points out, this creates two possible scenarios; one in which the feeling has gone, and a second where the feeling is still there but is somehow no longer a problem.

If a client states what will *not* be happening once the miracle happens – for example, she won't be worried any longer – the therapist needs to ask her what she will be doing *instead* of worrying.

Therapist: So what would you be doing differently if you were feeling more relaxed and happier now that the miracle has happened?
Client: I'd be getting on with my partner.
Therapist: So how would the day start and how would you notice things were different?
Client: We'd get up together and if it wasn't a work day we'd spend some time planning what we were going to do together.
Therapist: So what else would be happening?

The phrase 'what else' is a recurring one in SFT as practitioners use it to obtain detailed answers to questions such as scaling, the miracle question and exception seeking. When you can't think what else to say, say what else! Clients may want to explore more than one answer to the miracle question, for example, what the miracle would look like if they stayed in the relationship or what it would look like if they ended it. Therapists unfamiliar with solution-focused methods often have difficulty in exploring the answer to the miracle question in sufficient detail. It is important to develop the skills of drawing the client out because the quality of the answer in terms of its specificity and concreteness is crucial for the construction of the solution.

Client: He'd be able to take criticism without getting angry.
Therapist: Would you be giving it differently because you were feeling
    more relaxed and happy?

The miracle question aims to reveal how the client can act to
improve the situation. In this exchange the therapist suggests that
the client will need to act differently to help bring about a more
peaceful relationship.

Client: Probably yes, a little bit more subtly.
Therapist: Would you try and do it more diplomatically, a bit calmer?
    You wouldn't be shouting or something like that?
Client: No.
Therapist: And he would take it better?
Client: Yes, because that's the only way things are going to be solved,
    by talking about things.

The therapist explores the unique strategies this client would
adopt to change her problematic behaviour. The client has
already suggested that she knows what to do but it is helpful to
encourage her to describe exactly what she would do. The
therapist occupies a 'one down' (non-expert) position, curious to
know what the client has in mind.

Therapist: So if things were a lot better you'd both be sitting down and
    you'd be able to communicate more clearly without upsetting each
    other and say what it is you'd like to happen, what you would like
    him to do, what he would like you to do. So what would you be
    talking about?
Client: Probably about me having some more help with the kids. If I
    ask him to do anything he just says he's too busy, but he comes
    round later if I leave him alone.

Typically clients swing between solution and problem talk. The
therapist listens and empathises but does not expand problem
talk unless it is apparent that the client needs to explain a
situation. There is also no point in the therapist remaining on
solution territory when the client is back on problem terrain.

Therapist: So, if you were really handling it just the way you'd like,
    you'd be able to say about getting help without him feeling . . .
Client: That I'm getting at him.
Therapist: How do you do it at the moment? What would need to
    happen for you to do that again?

Having identified with the client a desired change in behaviour,
the therapist now seeks to find out which strategies may help to
bring about this change. There is a specific interest in current

successful strategies which the client could develop. In the first instance the therapist tries to find out whether any existing strategies are working. If they are working, the client might consider how to maintain or even extend them; if they are not working, she needs to think about discarding them and doing something different. When clients feel that nothing is working and that they have tried everything, the therapist needs to be supportive and empathic and not pressurise the client into being more optimistic. Believing that the client is co-operating as best she can, the therapist will not force the pace but will move at the client's tempo.

Clients often become animated and energetic when answering the miracle question. It often feels as though the atmosphere in the session has changed and that there is more energy in the room. Solution talk also seems to encourage a therapeutic use of humour in which both parties enjoy laughing at some aspects of the situation. Publicly expressing their hopes in the miracle answer can in itself help to motivate people towards their goals. Clients often report how surprised they were by their answers to the miracle question.

The therapist helps the client to develop answers to the miracle question by active listening, prompting, empathising and therapeutic questioning. He does this:

1   By inviting the client to describe in detail the day after the miracle and by exploring how the differences in one part of the day will affect the other.

   Therapist: So when things go much better at work, what will it be like when you come home in the evening?
   Therapist: When you manage to handle the children better during the day, what will be happening in the evening?

2   By asking questions about other significant people and how the miracle would affect them.

- Who will be the first person in the family to notice a miracle has happened? How will they react?
- What difference will that make to you?
- How will you know that they have found out?
- How will your partner behave now that the miracle has happened?

Questions may focus on feelings as well as behaviour:

- How will you feel if you manage to do that?

Is it always appropriate to use the miracle question? Some practitioners advocate caution when using it in situations where it could be insensitive, for example, when the person has a terminal illness or has suffered a recent bereavement. These are situations when the most likely answer to the miracle question is something unattainable, such as a bereaved person wanting the return of the dead person. Some therapists would customise the question in such a way as to rule out this answer which they feel would be unhelpful for the client. Others prefer to 'work with what you've got' and argue that much helpful information can come from the question even in these circumstances (Butler and Powers 1996). For some clients a modified form of the miracle question might feel more appropriate. Possible alternative versions might be:

- If you were aiming to bring about change in this area of your life, what would be the first signs you were making progress?
- If you went into work tomorrow (went to school, home or wherever the problem takes place) and all your problems were solved, what would have happened?
- Suppose you were starting (your job, this relationship or whatever) again, what things would you like to be different?
- If you came to work (home, school) tomorrow and the situation that was causing you distress had been removed, what do you think you would notice?

The miracle question is also a powerful tool in couple and family therapy. Each member offers his or her own version of life without the problem. This is often an enlightening experience for other family members. A variation is to use circular questioning to enable one client to predict how the other will answer the miracle question. The ensuing discussion can help to move on people who have been stuck in blaming, negative and critical frames of mind. In conflict situations the therapist tries to highlight the common ground, modify unreasonable demands and compliment the parties on what they are doing already to solve the problem.

Failed solutions

Identifying patterns of failed solutions is the characteristic of the MRI form of brief problem-focused therapy. Some solution-focused therapists include elements of this perspective in their repertoire. The therapist believes that, in order to do something different from what he is currently doing to deal with the problem, the client needs to abandon 'solutions' which have failed repeatedly in the past. Some clients find it useful to hear about failed (as well as successful) solutions which other people in similar situations have tried, in order to learn from them.

EXAMPLE

> *Therapist*: One of my clients some time ago went through an experi-
> ence similar to the one you are going through now. He started
> staying up all night and drowning his sorrows in the hope that
> alcohol would help him to sleep. He became quite cut off from his
> family and found that it was very difficult for him to get back into a
> normal routine. It made it very difficult for him to get back to work.
> He also spent quite a lot of money on alcohol and this caused a lot
> of stress at home.

Many people, especially young people, want or indeed need to make their own mistakes in order to learn their own lessons. The therapist needs to be sensitive to the danger that such story-telling could be seen as patronising and even moralising by the client.

At the end of a successful course of therapy, a solution-focused therapist might ask the client what she thinks would be useful for future clients with similar problems to know. Often clients have ideas or tips to pass on which the therapist would never have thought of. The therapist can dip into this fund of hard-earned wisdom by keeping good case notes or by keeping a file of therapeutic tips for clients.

The outcomes of therapy are the clients' goals. As soon as possible, the therapist explores with the client how to achieve them and in what order of priority. During and after each session, the therapist evaluates with the client whether what they are doing together is proving helpful. If it is proving helpful, they continue along the same lines and if it is not, the therapist needs to do something different.

Scaling in a first session

When words fail, numbers can come to our rescue. Given the complexity of human communications, we frequently fail to grasp the other person's meaning. We may assume we know what they are talking about, but often this assumption proves to be unfounded. De Shazer and his colleagues (de Shazer and Berg 1992) began to use scaling in their work as they found that clients could use it to express what they meant, even if the meaning was not clear to anyone else.

The therapist uses a scale of zero to ten, with ten representing the morning after the miracle and zero representing rock bottom, the worst the problem has been (or perhaps how the client felt before contacting the service). The primary purpose of scaling questions is to help clients set small identifiable goals, measure progress (beginning, middle and end) and establish priorities for action. They are also used to assess client motivation and confidence; in fact, they can be used with virtually any aspect of the therapy process. They can be attached to metaphors or images:

- If your problem feels like a ten-ton weight on you at the moment, what would it feel like if it was down to nine tons and how would you have got rid of that one ton?

They are invariably introduced in first sessions and developed subsequently. Scaling is a practical tool which a client can use between sessions. The use of numbers is purely arbitrary but it is client-centred. It is unwise for a therapist to assume that she knows what the client is aiming for or will accept. Contrary to expectation, most clients do not yearn for the moon but rather want small but appreciable improvements in their life.

The following is an excerpt from a first interview in which the client reports that she and her partner have separated and are considering divorce.

EXAMPLE

    Client: He says that he wants me to go back to him.
    Therapist: On a scale of zero to ten, ten being you are absolutely sure you want to go back and zero being it's absolutely out of the question, where do you feel you are at the moment?
    Client: About six and that's being generous considering how he's treated me. If you had asked me last week I would have said one.

The client is making three points here:

- My sense of trust is in a state of flux and could go up or down.
- I have managed to change my attitude or behaviour, despite feeling low.
- I have changed in the direction of us getting back together again.

This change has not been without cost and she might need a period in which she consolidates her six.

> *Therapist*: How did you get from one to six?
> *Client*: It's helped just getting away from him for a few days. I asked him to stop pestering me with phone calls and letters and he has. I've also been remembering how hard a time he's been through as well, losing his job. Maybe we both need help. He never talks to anyone.

The client demonstrates her commitment to tackling the problem. She is taking time to think through the problem as well as trying to see things from his point of view.

> *Therapist*: How did you manage to do that? It was a big jump for you getting to six wasn't it?
> *Client*: I think perhaps because I know that this might be our last chance. We can't carry on the way we were, it's got to change one way or another. If we can agree on a few things I would be willing to give it a last try.
> *Therapist*: What do you think you are doing differently because it feels like a last chance this time?
> *Client*: I've stopped criticising him in front of the children. When he's asked to see them, I haven't made it difficult. If we're going to get back together, he's got to get on better with the kids.
> *Therapist*: What do you think he is on the scale in terms of wanting to come back?
> *Client*: About the same. I think we're both a little bit unsure of one another at the moment.

Scales can be useful in working with not only the perceptions of the identified client, but also with those of partners/friends/colleagues.

> *Therapist*: You're both at six now, is that good enough for you to start living together again or do you need to get to seven or what?
> *Client*: I think we need to be six for longer before he should come back.
> *Therapist*: What would need to happen to keep you both at six for the next week or two?

Client: He needs to show me he's serious about giving me the support I need.

Therapist: What would be the first signs for you that he was getting better at that?

Client: He would listen to me when I tell him what I'm feeling and not be so selfish in the way he always puts himself first. He thinks it's all right for him to go on about his problems, but as soon as I start telling him how hard it's been at home with the kids, he doesn't want to know.

Therapist: So you'll feel more confident about being a six when he starts to listen to you more than he does at the moment. Anything else?

Client: He'll let me know where he is and not come home at all hours of the night.

Therapist: What difference would that make for you?

Client: I'd trust him more, at the moment I don't know what he's up to.

The discussion about how to keep at six elicits a description of the observable behaviour which the client wants from her partner. When the client expresses what she wants in negative terms (what will not be happening), the therapist rephrases it in positive terms (what will be happening instead).

Assessing motivation

> A dream without a vision is a day dream, a vision without a dream is a nightmare.

> Origins unknown

We tend to work towards goals of our own choosing. When others set goals for us we might comply out of duress or politeness, but we often find many ways to sabotage them. One of the strengths of solution-focused work is the way in which it stays very close to the client's own goals and does not try to convert them to something else.

EXAMPLE

Therapist: On a scale of zero to ten, ten being you would do anything to overcome these panic attacks and zero being you would really love to but you don't think you will do anything, where would you put yourself today?

Client: Three.

Therapist: Will three be good enough to make a start?

Client: No. I feel I've tried everything and nothing works. I've almost given up hope that it could get any better.

Therapist: So although you've had a lot of setbacks you've managed to keep trying? Some people would have completely given up, how have you kept going?

Client: We've always been fighters in my family. My mum taught me to keep at it when things weren't going well.

Therapist: So if she was here she would say keep fighting?

Client: Yes.

Therapist: Where would you need to get to on the scale before you felt you had a chance of fighting off the panic attacks?

Client: Five.

Therapist: How will you know when you've got to five?

Client: If I could relax more. I feel so tense most of the time, it keeps giving me headaches and then I feel like giving up.

Therapist: How would you go about being relaxed enough to feel you were getting to five?

Client: I don't know.

Therapist: When the sun comes out for you and you feel less tense than usual what has helped to make you better?

Client: When I'm on my own and I can listen to my own music.

Therapist: Anything else?

Client: I like Fridays when I don't have to go to work. I can lie in and potter around a bit.

Therapist: Does that mean that if this Friday you put on your music and had an easy start to the day, you'd probably feel a five and more able to fight back against the panic attacks?

Client: I think so.

Therapist: If you're a three today, what would help to get you to be a four?

Similar questions may explore the client's level of confidence in relation to the problem.

Discovering the client's resources

Competence seeking

The therapist sets out to discover and affirm the resources, strengths and qualities which the client can utilise to 'solve' the problem (de Shazer 1988). It is not enough to identify resources, it is necessary to understand how they were deployed and how to reactivate them. The current problem situation may differ from previous ones in which the client coped, but there is often an identifiable pattern, for example, the client's previous experience of loss.

A client who felt suicidal after the death of her mother, experienced similar thoughts and feelings on the breakdown of her marriage. With the therapist she recalled how she had coped with her grief and considered how she might use those resources again.

We know that many people with psychological problems are 'spontaneous improvers' and that most people do not have recourse to professional help when they experience problems in life. Such people adapt to the problems their environment creates by using skills, beliefs, character qualities and social networks, as and when needed. In solution-focused work we seek to bring those resources into the awareness of the client. This does not mean that clients possess fully formed solutions 'within themselves', but that they have the potential to solve their own problems. They may need a therapist to help them own and apply their resources, or extend or modify their existing repertoire of life skills.

Exception seeking
The therapist engages the client in seeking exceptions to the problem – that is, those times when the problem was not present or was being managed better. Chevalier (1995) makes a useful distinction between deliberate and spontaneous exceptions.

Deliberate exceptions take place when people do something which they can see made a difference to the problem and which they feel capable of repeating. What they did or stopped doing was an experiment, but it altered the problem situation for the better and would be worth trying again. This need not mean that the client repeat exactly what worked last time there was an exception. The circumstances may have changed so that mere repetition is no longer appropriate. Mechanically repeating actions may even be part of the problem!

EXAMPLE

Jim was very clear that he needed a range of techniques to use when he had panic attacks. He knew that for him nothing worked for very long. He developed a hierarchy of strategies to use depending on the severity of the attack. For him it was important to know that he had mental (recite the alphabet backwards, for example), physical (relaxed breathing), psychological (self-talk) and visual (picturing himself as strong and coping) strategies which he could vary to meet the challenge at the time.

Spontaneous exceptions are those occasions when, for some mysterious reason or for some reason beyond the person's control, the problem did not happen or was not as bad as it usually is. The client does not feel that this had anything to do with her or believes that it was due to certain circumstances which are unlikely to be repeated. As far as the client is concerned, they were welcome surprises but these incidents have nothing to contribute to solving the problem. They were insignificant exceptions.

With deliberate exceptions the strategy would be to encourage the client to keep doing what worked and even expand upon it if that were possible. With spontaneous exceptions, one can still often extract some aspect of the exception which throws light on the solution.

EXAMPLE

Client: I've not been so stressed the past week.
Counsellor: How did you manage that?
Client: I was on holiday.
Counsellor: How did you manage to relax on your holiday?
Client: It was great being out of the hostile atmosphere. After a couple of days I really unwound and managed to forget about it. It's going to be hard going back.
Counsellor: How did you succeed in forgetting about work for a bit, that must have been difficult?
Client: It took me a while, but I was determined it was not going to ruin my holiday. I didn't leave a phone number so I couldn't be contacted and I told my partner to stop me if I started to talk shop.
Counsellor: So when you were able to switch off that helped. Do you ever manage to do that when you're at home?
Client: No, I feel work takes over my life.
Counsellor: As well as switching off, what else did you do that helped on holiday?
Client: Having some peace and quiet was wonderful. Not having people wanting something from me all the time. Having time for myself.
Counsellor: What did you enjoy most when you had time to yourself?
Client: I enjoyed doing nothing. I read some novels, which I haven't done for ages, and listened to some of my music.

Counsellor: So you know that finding time to be on your own, some-where relatively peaceful and quiet where you can just collapse or read or listen to music, really helps you to cope with stress.

Client: Yes, I wish I could take a long, long holiday!

Counsellor: Even if that were not possible, is there anything you did or did not do on holiday that you would like to keep doing, and if so, how could you ensure that it happens?

The exploration of exceptions should be as detailed as possible, without it becoming an oppressive interrogation. It should cover not only what the client did, but also how she was thinking, what self-talk was taking place and how she was feeling before, during and after the exception occurred. The response of other significant people to the exceptions can also be revealing. The therapist might ask: 'What difference did it make to your colleagues/partner/children when this exception took place?' Exceptions provide a glimpse of what the future could be like for the client and provide clues for tracking solutions, as well as discarding failed solutions. For clients used to professionals concentrating exclusively on their problems, this experience of mini-solution seeking can come as a welcome change. It affirms competence, increases confidence and motivation, and raises the level of optimism and hope. Quick (1994) describes the therapist asking a client if she has noticed whether her distress varies in intensity. If she says that it does, the therapist then asks the client if she is aware of how she manages to make that happen. The client may not know the answer, but the seed has been sown that she is or is not doing (thinking, feeling) something that affects the level of her distress.

White (1989) describes exceptions as 'unique outcomes' which tell alternative stories about the client. Clients often have strongly developed problem-focused narratives but underdeveloped solution narratives. By encouraging an over-elaboration of the problem-focused narrative, the client can come to feel less and less able to change her 'problem identity' by herself and more dependent on the therapist to do it for her. In SFT the therapist facilitates the generation of alternative solution stories which orient the person towards a new affirming identity. Eliciting exceptions does not always produce immediate results. If, when you are learning to drive, you stall the car each time you try to start it, you tend to dismiss the one time you moved off smoothly as an inexplicable aberration (beginner's luck!). As the frequency of the exceptions increases and becomes the rule, attention moves to the next problem area – reversing round corners! After a while you forget you ever had a problem with starting.

Exploring tasks

The message
SFT clients will know from pre-therapy information that towards the end of each session the workers will take a short break in order to compose the feedback, or 'the message', as it is known in SFT. If there is no co-worker, the therapist may still take a break and leave the room, or she may stay in the room but, with the permission of the client, take a couple of minutes to reflect on what has been said and to prepare the feedback. If a client is distressed or excessively anxious the therapist may decide to omit the break altogether. However, in my experience most clients cope well with the break. Sometimes they are mentally and emotionally tired by the end of the session and actually welcome the space to collect themselves. In preparing to take the break, the therapist reminds the client about it and asks whether there is anything else the client would like to tell the therapist.

Typically, the first part of the message is a compliment given to the client, acknowledging what he is doing or thinking about the problem which is proving to be constructive. This ensures that the client receives the credit for the efforts he has already made to overcome personal and environmental difficulties. If the client has been in therapy for some time there will hopefully be many examples of this. The giving of compliments, in a non-patronising way, helps to reduce the power gap between the client and the therapist and often increases the sense of collaboration between them. Genuine compliments, as distinct from manipulative flattery, help to motivate people, especially those with long experience of failure and isolation. We have all experienced the encouragement which an unexpected compliment gives. In therapy, the compliment has to be given with sensitivity to the needs of the individual client and, where appropriate, it has to take into account gender and cultural issues. Often the therapist will express appreciation for the co-operation which the client has shown in the session. If it proves difficult to find anything constructive to feed back, one can at least compliment the client on having the courage to come and explore the use of therapy.

The second stage is for the therapist to summarise any positive strategies which the client has already begun to use, or those which he intends to implement in the future. The therapist will usually encourage the client to consolidate what is already proving to be helpful. The following is an excerpt from a message delivered to a client who had been suffering from stress.

EXAMPLE

> *Therapist*: What has really impressed both of us today has been you knowing your own mind. . . . You've actually developed a degree of self-awareness which . . . is giving you a lot of knowledge about yourself. . . . That knowledge you're translating into behaviour so that as you become aware of a situation . . . you're actually telling yourself 'I don't have to follow the old script. I can do this differently. I don't have to go from zero to sixty in five seconds'. . . . I think you've developed some techniques for preventing problems building up . . . from the way you can register automatic thoughts but not let them overpower you . . . I think one of the things you're really trying to do is to move down a gear and usually when you move down a gear you get more control of the car. You've learnt to slow down.

As well as encouraging the client to keep doing what is beginning to work, the therapist may invite the client to carry out a task. A task is a clear, agreed and collaboratively designed step which the client is going to take between sessions. It could be a suggestion for the client to think about something, to do something or to notice something. The latter is an invitation to the client to look for evidence of particular types of 'solution' behaviour and report them back to the therapist. It is often the case that people only begin to notice things when they need to pay attention to them.

Formula first session task
This task, known as the formula first session task (FFST), is usually given to a client at the end of the initial meeting, irrespective of what the problem is. It is, to use de Shazer's (1985) phrase, a 'skeleton key' intervention. The standard formula is:

> Until the next time we meet, I'd like you just to observe what things are happening in your life/family/work that you'd like to see continue, then come back and tell me about it.

A study by Adams, Piercy and Jurich (1991) of the FFST, as given to family therapy clients, some of whom received a single SFT session, indicated that it was an effective intervention for gaining compliance, increasing the clarity of therapeutic goals and initiating improvement in the presenting problem. Clients were more likely to perform the 'solution-focused' task than a control group given a 'problem-focused' task. The former returned for a second session reporting clearer goals and improvement in the presenting problem. Although there was an immediate impact from the FFST, it did not influence the outcome of treatment measured at the tenth session or at termination, whichever came first.

The FFST is an invitation to clients to act in a forward-looking, constructive and change-oriented way. They may not feel very positive, but they can still look for what they want to see continue without there being any pressure to do anything different. The purpose of the task is to broaden the client's problem-centred outlook in order to encompass those parts of their lives which are exceptions to the problem. If the client can find this type of evidence, even in embryonic form, it breaks the rigid problem mould and raises the possibility of change. The clear expectation communicated by the therapist is that change is there to be found. This in itself can help to create a 'self-fulfilling prophecy'. The therapist may request the client to perform this 'fact-finding mission' in order to help the therapist obtain a clearer picture of exactly what is happening in the client's life, so that the therapist can help the client more effectively.

The content of the first session, although characterised by the interventions described here, is of course individually tailored to the client's needs. While one first session might include pre-session change, the miracle question and scaling, another might employ only some of these.

5

Second Sessions and Beyond

If not you, who? If not now, when?

Rabbi Hillel, cited in Hoyt (1995)

What makes this a problem? Why now?

Slive, MacLaurin, Oakander and Amundson (1995)

In describing second and subsequent sessions, I feel compelled to issue the same therapeutic health warning as given at the start of the last chapter. Textbook clients do not exist and counsellors are not automatons. Each client has a unique combination of needs and abilities; for some, change can be sudden and dramatic, while for others it is slow and tortuous. The outline of a second session is only a guide, not a definitive version. The model serves the client, not the client the model. There is no mechanical formula. O'Hanlon and Weiner-Davis (1989: 77) graphically describe the therapeutic process as:

> a bit like rock climbing. You have an idea of the goal, but the actual scaling of the mountain involves using general methods of rock climbing adapted to a particular mountain. Sometimes you may even have to break the rule of the accepted method to reach the goal. The mountain will 'teach' you how to scale it. Likewise, clients have taught us how to help them reach their goals and sometimes they have taught us that it will take something other than our usual procedures to get there.

Aims of the second session

In co-operation with the client, the aims of second and subsequent sessions are:

- To consolidate constructive change.
- To review task performance, where appropriate.

- To construct the solution.
- To develop new strategies for change.
- To continue to deconstruct the problem.
- To evaluate the counselling and plan ending.

These aims are not self-contained, they overlap each other. The order above reflects not so much a sequence to follow, but the priority of focusing on solutions rather than problems. Some solution-focused counsellors start the second session by asking: 'What's better or what's different?' Others adopt a less direct approach and accept that the client is likely to want to report on the week past, with its successes and its failures. If the client needs to engage in further discussion of the problem, it is important to listen with respect and attentiveness. The client may need to retell stories or provide new ones until he feels sure that the counsellor understands. As the counsellor listens, she is able to hear how the client constructs his world. At the same time, the conversation enables the client to 'reality test' possible future courses of action. In listening to the client it may be possible to ask coping and scaling questions from the very start, as long as it does not feel to the client that the problem is being trivialized or that the counsellor is being oppressively optimistic.

Consolidating constructive change

'The purpose of each successive session is to assess change and to help to maintain it so that a solution can be achieved' (Lipchik and de Shazer 1986). This climate of change needs also to be an environment which feels safe, respectful and validating for the client. The constructivist view that people create meaning for their own lives fosters a climate of experimentation in which the counsellor encourages the client to explore different ways of viewing and acting in relation to the problem. This is similar to the personal construct view of the client as a scientist who conducts experiments in living. The counsellor invites the client to share her curiosity as to what might happen next.

It is important that the client feels able to report failure as well as success. Clients sometimes try to please the counsellor by making only positive reports, but it would be counterproductive for a counsellor to evoke or reinforce only the successes of the client. There is also a tension between the client initially experiencing a relationship of unconditional positive regard, and the change in dynamics after the counsellor has asked the client to carry out a between-session task. From that point on, even if the counsellor does not challenge the client as to whether the task was performed or not, an element of conditionality has entered into the approval the counsellor offers the client. The counsellor cannot avoid having feelings about whether the client performed the task agreed or not. And the client's feelings about the counsellor will change because he is trying to gain approval or, if the task is too stressful or difficult, he will experience feelings of anger and anxiety, resentment, fear of failure and in some cases will withdraw from the relationship. Janis (1983: 33) sums up the dilemma for the counsellor:

> Unless a counsellor . . . elicits some degree of commitment to carry out a course of action, the clients are likely to remain relatively unaffected and will derive little benefit from the relationship as far as the common goals of counselling are concerned. If the practitioner makes no such demands, either explicitly or implicitly, the relationship of the client to the accepting counsellor will continue in a warm, friendly way but will be ineffectual. Here is another of those human conditions where love is not enough.

Clients often make progress following an initial interview. This may be due in part to the relief which comes from unburdening one's concerns, and possibly secrets, to another human being. The act of seeking help may in itself restore a sense of power and control in the client's life. Talmon's (1990) research into single sessions demonstrates the power of a first session, showing how it can promote new thinking and behaviour in clients and how, despite the scepticism of many counsellors, it can meet the treatment goals clients have. The solution-focused counsellor sets out to discover how clients managed to make changes, however small, and how they might maintain or extend them. If the client reports positive change, the counsellor will offer encouragement and compliments: 'that couldn't have been easy/it sounds as if you handled that really well/how did you manage to do it?/not many people could have done what you've done/I'm very pleased that you think you're getting things under control.' How this feedback is delivered is as important as the actual content. The manner of delivery will vary according to the personality and circumstances of the client, with a celebratory tone being appropriate in some instances but not in others. It is important for therapeutic momentum that clients accept credit for the changes which they have made and that they do not attribute progress solely to the counsellor, or to some freak circumstance. The client's response to constructive change may be indicative of her position on a continuum of pessimism/optimism; passivity/action; self-criticism/self-affirmation; dependence/independence. The pacing and timing of interventions will need to take these factors into account.

Clients may feel ambivalent about the changes which they are contemplating or which they have already made. Change usually entails losses as well as gains. Some clients may choose to live with the status quo because the price of change is too high. Others, in their desperation to escape a painful situation, may make changes which they are unable to sustain, or which produce short-term benefits but prove to be destructive in the long term. Some people want cast-iron guarantees that the changes will bring the desired result, while others procrastinate because they are seeking the perfect solution, which of course does not exist.

The counsellor helps clients to consolidate change by asking questions about what is working and how small changes could be maintained or amplified. These could be summarised as maintenance, learning and evaluation strategies as described in Figure 5.1.

Many clients express their therapeutic goal as acquiring a better understanding of themselves and their problems. This is despite knowing from experience that being able to answer the question why a problem happens does not automatically reveal how to solve it. Knowing intellectually how to solve a problem does not always motivate us to act. In fact, it can allow us to retreat into rationalisations of the status quo. Anyone who has fought against an unwanted habit, whether it be food, cigarettes, alcohol or anything else, has experienced the gulf between intellectual understanding and ability to act. Solution-focused therapy (SFT) suggests to clients that new awareness can result from *acting* differently in relation to their problem and that experiential learning can be more valuable and powerful than insight alone: 'learning to be the person you want to be is quite different – and often less time-consuming – than learning why you are the

- *Maintenance strategies*   What needs to happen for the changes to keep happening? What might stop you from doing that? How would you overcome those obstacles? What would be worth doing again (perhaps in a slightly different way)? (Watzlawick, Weakland and Fisch 1974). What do you think you need to keep going? What will be the first thing you do once you see the signs of the problem returning? Who could be on your side to help you with some or all of this?

- *Learning strategies*   How did you decide to do that? What do you think that says about you? (White 1988) What have you learned from what you have tried so far? What have you learned to stop doing? How will you manage to stop yourself doing it again? What will be the gains for you when you abandon your 'failed solutions'? What have you thought about doing instead? How will you be able to remind yourself of what you've learned if the problem arises again? Are there any strategies which you are thinking of experimenting with? Are there some aspects of the problem which you feel you have to live with and others which you think you need to change?

- *Evaluation strategies*   Are you finding this therapy helpful, is it making a difference? Are the changes along the lines that you want? Is your goal the same or has it altered? What should we be doing more or less of? Is there something that's missing that you think I should know about? What else do I need to know in order to help you more?

  In particular, the counsellor will use scaling questions.

Figure 5.1   *Counsellor strategies*

way you are' (Fanger 1993). We often understand the past more easily by reflecting on the present and the future, than on direct historical investigations. The client's request for understanding must be treated with respect as failure to do so may result in a loss of rapport and co-operation.

Research indicates that the maximum impact of counselling takes place in the first six to eight sessions (Koss and Butcher 1986). In brief counselling, where time is rationed, there are less opportunities to recover from an unproductive start; hence the importance of early and ongoing evaluation by the two parties and a willingness on the part of the counsellor to change what she is doing if it is found to be unhelpful. The solution-focused approach is a pragmatic one in which the counsellor experiments with different interventions depending on whether they are or not helping the client to move towards his goals. If the client is not making progress, there may be a review of how the problem has been constructed, a reappraisal of the client's goals or a change of pace by the counsellor.

Reviewing task performance

Solution-focused counsellors vary in the importance which they attach to giving tasks and inviting clients to report on task performance. In the early years of SFT task giving occupied a more central role than it does today. The emphasis has since moved from the counsellor prescribing tasks, to support for clients in tasks which they themselves have designed. There is arguably a greater likelihood that clients will perform solution-oriented tasks they have initiated themselves, rather than those proposed by someone else, although some clients might respond more readily to a request from an authority figure. In practice, some clients are less compliant than others and will modify any counsellor proposal or devise their own tasks. James was given the task of worrying about his problem for fifteen minutes every day in an attempt to reduce the amount of time he wasted worrying about his problems. He carried out the task for three days, then got bored and decided it would be more productive to spend the time thinking about what he could do to solve his problems. When he reported this to the counsellor, he was congratulated and encouraged to continue to pursue his own ideas about what was most helpful for him.

De Shazer (1996) advises against giving a client another task if he fails to accomplish a set task. The counsellor may congratulate the client for knowing that the time was not right to do what he had been asked. How will he know that the time is right for him to act? What, if anything, did he do instead? Some clients devise their own task that is different from the one suggested by the counsellor. Rather than give a negative connotation to this, the counsellor is more likely to congratulate the client on knowing best what to do in the situation. Non-compliance may be a sign of therapeutic health. If the counsellor is planning to ask the client to carry out a task it is advisable to sound him out before the end of the session in case there are good reasons why the task is unrealistic or even impossible. The client may have already tried such a suggestion before and knows it does not work or that it has negative side-effects.

Not all clients welcome the idea of homework. Some feel that nothing will make a difference, that everything has been tried and failed. They may feel like passive victims who can only suffer in silence or in a state of 'learned helplessness'. But being resigned to a problem still implies a degree of coping behaviour. It is impossible to do nothing. There are always elements in their coping strategies on which the counsellor could build.

Since many clients will have received the formula first session task to do – 'please notice and come back and tell me things which you would like to see continue in your life' – the second session often begins with the client reporting back the answers to this purposefully vague task. The answers often help to redress the problem-centred view of life the client has held and help to identify pieces of the solution jigsaw.

Constructing the solution

In SFT the counsellor invests a great deal of time and energy in helping the client to focus in a concrete and detailed way on the various elements in the solution, namely those changes which the client has stated he wants to bring about. In second sessions and subsequently the counsellor focuses on the following solutions.

Revisiting the miracle question
Clients can change their answers to the original miracle question. They may decide that one part of the 'miracle' scenario is already happening, without actually waiting for a miracle. Or they may decide that, on reflection, they do not want the miracle or some aspect of it.

Predictions
Predictions (Kral and Kowalski 1989) are quite often utilised in SFT, particularly with clients who report that change happens randomly and cannot, therefore, be repeated. They can help to tease out which behaviours constitute the changes the client would like and how they came about on a particular occasion. The counsellor might invite the client to predict each evening whether tomorrow is going to be a good or a bad day. At the end of the day the client checks his prediction for its accuracy. If it was accurate, the client tries to identify what shaped the day. If the prediction was inaccurate, the client might discover the positive experiences which made it a better day than expected; or if the day was worse than predicted, try to identify the trouble spots which might be avoidable, at least to some extent, in the future. According to Berg (1991), clients tend, at least initially, to

predict more bad days than they actually have. The exploration of predictions can become a valuable learning experience for clients.

Exploring past suggestions

The counsellor may also explore with a client not only solutions which have been attempted in the past, but ones which were proposed or suggested in the past but not actually used. Understanding why he did not act on the suggestion at that time can be another useful piece of learning for the client. It may emerge that the suggested course of action was (and still is) a sensible one, but the client rejected it because of the source from which it came. In new circumstances the client might be willing to revise his earlier decision.

Scaling

In second and subsequent sessions the counsellor uses scaling questions to monitor progress and set goals. It is a form of fine tuning of the therapeutic process which enables the client and the counsellor to sense the direction in which the work is going. It ensures that the counsellor stays close to the client's agenda for change. As in the first session, the use of numbers is a self-regulating activity which the client uses to symbolise his relationship to the problem. Many clients find this way of talking helpful because it assists them to discuss the solution picture in small manageable pieces. Instead of the problem feeling like a mountain, it can be scaled down to a series of climbable hills with each step plotted along the way. Scaling is a tool which clients can, and frequently do, use between sessions.

At the second session the counsellor will normally ask the client how he is managing with the problem on a scale of zero to ten, zero representing either the starting point in counselling or a time when the problem was at its worst and ten a time when the problem is solved. It is a common experience that clients' first response to this question is: 'Nothing has changed, everything's the same.' It is a mistake for the counsellor to accept this as the client's last word on the matter. When the counsellor makes further enquiries – 'Our first session was last Wednesday, how were things on Thursday . . . Friday . . . Saturday?' – the answers become more discriminating.

EXAMPLE

Client: Friday wasn't too bad.
Counsellor: What was happening on Friday?
Client: I managed to sleep better than I've been doing.
Counsellor: What difference did that make to you during the day?
Client: I was able to work better and I wasn't feeling so down all the time.
Counsellor: What else was different on Friday?
Client: Because I wasn't so tired all day, I was in a better mood and I wasn't snapping at my partner all the time.
Counsellor: So on a scale of zero to ten, ten being everything was perfect, what were you on Friday?
Client: Six.
Counsellor: Would it be all right if you were six every day?
Client: It would be all right to be six most of the time, but as long as I had some days when I was higher than that, eight or nine.
Counsellor: What would it take for you to have two days next week which were six?
Client: Get to bed early and get a good night's sleep would be a start.
Counsellor: Anything else?
Client: Make myself some proper meals and cut down on my drinking.
Counsellor: How could you do that?

Consolidating progress is at least as important as making it in the first place.

EXAMPLE

Client: I've had a really bad week. I feel like I'm back at square one again.
Counsellor: So where would you say you were on the scale today?
Client: Minus five.
Counsellor: How long do you think you will stay at minus five before you move up or down?
Client: I don't know. It all depends. If I could only learn to say no when my boss asks me to take on more work, everything would be fine.
Counsellor: If you managed just once to say no, you think it would make a big difference?
Client: Yes.
Counsellor: When will you know you're ready to move from minus five and start moving up the scale again?
Client: I'm ready now. I don't want to feel as bad as this again. Things have got to get better.
Counsellor: What will be the first signs for you that you're beginning to fight back?
Client: When I stop taking work home with me.
Counsellor: How could you do that?

The counsellor may also explore through scaling what the client is doing to stop the situation deteriorating.

EXAMPLE

> *Counsellor*: I know it's been a bad week, but how did you stop it from being even worse?
> *Client*: I went out with my friend on Friday and we had a good talk. It helped me to face Monday. I don't know how I would cope if I couldn't lean on her.
> *Counsellor*: So she's important to you. What else do you do or stop doing when you manage to stop the slide?
> *Client*: I tell myself I'm a lot better than I was a year ago. I know I'm not as much of a doormat as I used to be. I think of all I've been through and survived.
> *Counsellor*: So when you get negative self-critical thoughts, you answer back by remembering how strong you must have been to come through what you did.
> *Client*: Yes.
> *Counsellor*: How do you remind yourself of that?

Clients might report that they are better but not in relation to the problem area itself. They may see no connection between these improvements and the original problem. They may also report that the original problem is solved, but 'things' are still not better. In either case the counsellor has to renegotiate the focus of the work.

Developing or reinforcing strategies for change

> If we do not change our direction we are likely to end up where we are headed.
>
> Chinese proverb

The counsellor builds on what the client is doing already to help her take the next small step towards her goal. That step may be towards making further progress, to maintain progress already made or to halt further deterioration. What does the counsellor do when clients report no progress or deterioration?

It is important not to focus too much on setbacks. The counsellor may even have warned the client of possible relapses. Failure can provide opportunities for learning. At the very least the client can eliminate one course of action from the list of possible solutions. A relapse or setback can help to throw into clearer relief what the solution might look like. What made the situation worse might give a clue as to what would make it better. The counsellor may ask the client:

- Do you need to do something different?
- Are your goals realistic?
- Is the timetable realistic?
- What did you do to stop it getting worse?
- How did you cope despite the problem not improving?

In some cases the problem recedes (temporarily or permanently) into the background and something else, either another problem or something positive, comes to the fore. Some clients move from one crisis to another, perhaps needing the drama and sense of being alive that brings. If one can help the client to identify what it is he gets from such experiences, it may be possible to explore problem-free ways of getting the same thing.

Underestimating the client's capacity for change
As counsellors we can hold clients back by lacking faith and trust in their ability to make changes in their lives. Although incremental change may prove most often to be a wise course of action, there are occasions when clients are ready for major changes and excessive caution or pessimism on the part of the counsellor can lead to them missing the optimum moment for change.

EXAMPLE

A female client presented at the first session with depression. She was currently off work sick. She felt guilty that she was neglecting her children. When she returned the following week she had managed to cook a meal for her two children every day after school, had helped them with their homework three times, and had visited her place of work to renegotiate her job. The counsellor expressed surprise that she had done so much in one week, and asked how she had managed it. Her reply was that she had not intended to do all of these things, but had decided to take control and make a start and one thing had led to another.

Deconstructing the problem

White (1993: 34) defines deconstruction as:

> procedures that subvert taken-for-granted realities and practices: those
> so-called 'truths' that are split off from the conditions and the context
> of their production; those disembodied ways of speaking that hide
> their biases and prejudices; and those familiar practices of self and of
> relationship that are subjugating people's lives.

There is often a fine line between joining the client in her
perceptions and unique experiences of her problem, and the
necessity at times to explore other interpretations of the situation,
other 'truths'. It is not in the spirit of SFT to do this in a confrontational, psycho-educational way, as one might find in some
of the cognitive therapies. It is often through contrasting the
clients' experience when exceptions happened with their original
definition of the problem that the problem itself becomes
redefined. It is important that the client's reframing is consistent
with her own values and viewpoints. Many clients have encoun-
tered professionals who have imposed their own ideological
framework on them.

The self-labelling which the client brings can be the end-
product of many years of searching for words to describe her
experience adequately. While having a diagnosis can be a source
of relief and reassurance in some circumstances, it can also be an
albatross around a person's neck. It can result in her living out
what she perceives to be typical behaviour for a person with that
label – it becomes a self-fulfilling prescription. The person will
feel ambivalent and threatened by possible changes to the status
quo. In solution-focused work the counsellor knows the power of
language to construct social reality and is conscious that the
problem is how something is talked about. The counsellor is
aware that he has his own constructions on the labels the client
uses to talk about the problem. He needs to question himself as
much as the client and be aware of his motivation in encouraging
her scepticism about the labels she has collected.

Being human, we seek to understand our life experiences,
although there are times when, as individuals and as a community, meaning eludes us and we are left with mystery. The
pace of life in contemporary society and the erosion of traditional
political, social and religious beliefs can leave people feeling that
they 'had the experience and missed the meaning'. The absence

of compelling meaning often lies at the heart of our personal troubles and anxieties. Our desire for meaning and purpose can lead us into a rigid and closed attitude to our experiences, so that we adopt a single filter through which we view the world. This narrowness may prove inadequate in the face of a rapidly changing and challenging environment. Our problems often result from the self-limiting restrictions imposed upon our view of life.

As counsellors we disclose the constructs, assumptions, biases and prejudices which comprise our own belief system as it meets the belief system of another human being. Yet despite these barriers, the purpose of the encounter is to create a bridge between counsellor and client which will enable the client to explore the meaning of his life. Understanding needs to be context-sensitive. In an archaeological dig, the meaning and purpose of a particular artifact can often only be discovered by a careful examination of its location with reference to all the other finds. If the pattern of relationships is lost or is unavailable for some reason, the meaning and purpose of the piece becomes obscure. Similarly, in the psychological field there are choices about meaning which are intrinsically linked to the context of the client's life.

There are various techniques a solution-focused counsellor uses to deconstruct the problem with a client.

Reframing
Reframing provides an alternative perspective on the problem. As Watzlawick puts it:

> To reframe means to change the conceptual and/or emotional setting or viewpoint in relation to which a situation is experienced and to place it in another frame which fits the 'facts' of the same concrete situation equally well or even better, and thereby changes its entire meaning. (Watzlawick, Weakland and Fisch 1974: 95)

An example of this would be indecision reframed as wise caution. While acknowledging the value of caution, particularly if it compensates for another person's impulsiveness (spontaneity), the counsellor can explore whether there are times when the client could allow herself to go off duty and be just a little less cautious for a while.

In the following exchange the two participants negotiate the meaning of crying.

EXAMPLE

> *Female client*: Since she died one thing I've done very little of is actually cry about it. I still don't think I can cry about it and I don't know whether that's odd or I just don't need to, I don't know. People keep telling me I would feel a lot better if I let it all out and there were one or two times I felt I would have liked to have sat down and had a good cry.
>
> *Counsellor*: Do you usually cry about other things?
>
> *Client*: No, I don't often cry when I'm upset.
>
> *Counsellor*: I guess people do what they need to do for themselves. Everyone's different and it might be interesting to think of how you would feel and what you would do differently after you did cry. But I don't feel that you have to think of yourself as needing to do that – 'there must be something wrong with me if I don't cry.' Everyone's different.

From a constructionist perspective, tears have many possible meanings, all of which are negotiable between the two parties. The client holds the dominant cultural belief that she ought to be able to cry about her loss and that she will not get better until she does. She feels anxious and odd because she is unable to cry like other people do. The counsellor explores the meaning which crying currently occupies in the client's life and offers the view that crying is an option but not a necessity for the client. He suggests that there is no one right way to express feelings. If the client accepts this she may feel released from the obligation to cry and this in turn will break the causal connection between having to cry and her recovery. Learning to cry in a culturally acceptable way (with strong gender expectations about the place crying occupies in the life of a woman) might be a very difficult thing for her to do and could require a lot of time to accomplish. In the meantime, counselling could be prolonged.

Externalisation

Externalisation of the problem is a form of reframing. It is a way of constructing a therapeutic conversation which locates the problem as being 'out there', not something within the person. It offers a different perspective from which the client can view his problem. Externalising the problem allows the possibility of the person shifting his attitude towards it. The client can, for example, have a greater sense of agency and power whereas previously there was a passive-victim stance. Talking about the problem as something which is 'in a relationship with' the client, rather than something the client 'is or has', changes the counsellor's approach to it. Instead of being the expert who has esoteric knowledge about the inner workings of the client's thoughts and feelings, there is a sense of 'joining with the client' in more of an outward than an inward journey.

EXAMPLE

Frank was subject to recurring bouts of depression. He was convinced that he had been 'hard wired' genetically to be a depressed person, just like his father. His depression was 'something' deep within him. This attitude contributed to a sense of fatalism and hopelessness in the face of this powerful condition. His depression prevented him from valuing anything good about himself or from noticing any times when he was less depressed. He was at a loss to explain how he had managed to come out of past depressions. His problem felt like a life sentence. With support, he was eventually able to externalise his depression as a force which attacked him from time to time and which overcame him, wrapping its gray blanket of gloom around him. This new way of looking at his feelings opened up new possibilities for learning to recognise the signs of an attack gathering, for knowing what he can do to defend himself, what works in fighting it off or what reduces the length or intensity of the attack. It also helped him to appreciate that there was a lot more to him than his problem. He had strengths, experiences, qualities, values and knowledge which he could utilise more in the fight against the depression. Depression is of course a terrible affliction which is not simply shaken off by an act of will power, but how the sufferer views it is an important element in his ability to recover from its worst effects.

Externalisation can also help to decrease conflict and blame about ownership of and responsibility for the problem. Without discounting accountability, it is possible to talk about the problem in a way which does not personalise it and thus invite blame, defensiveness and self-justification. It can help couples to face together the problem undermining their relationship, instead of playing a sterile game of blaming the other. It can open the door to alternative solutions (White and Epston 1990).

Testing constructs

The SFT counsellor may employ deconstructing strategies used in personal construct counselling. Kelly (1955) advocated a model of the person as a scientist who develops a hypothesis, predicts what might happen, then tests it out and evaluates the results. The counsellor may:

- Invite clients to test constructs for their predictive validity or internal consistency.
- Make more explicit the assumptions on which the constructs are being made.
- Invite the client to employ a different construct and experiment with it.

The counsellor challenges the client's viewing of the problem by commenting upon client thinking which:

- Exaggerates the problem and makes it very difficult to solve.
- Takes extreme, all-or-nothing positions and leaves little room for compromise or negotiation.
- Projects responsibility on to others. At some point the client needs to become a customer for change who takes ownership of some aspect of the problem.
- Sets unrealistic standards by aiming for perfection and dismisses 'good enough' as ever being a viable option.
- Makes tenuous or illogical connections between events. The client may see two associated events as causally connected.

In SFT the meaning of the client's experiences is negotiable, depending on the outcome of the linguistic transactions in which the client and therapist engage. The therapist adopts a 'not knowing' position in which he disowns the role of expert in the client's life. The purpose of the therapeutic dialogue is to negotiate jointly a meaning to the client's situation which will create the possibility of change for her. If talking about the problem appears to disempower the client, the therapist averts it by attempting to use other discourses which are potentially more open to change.

- How confident do you feel about following the plan?
- What will you need to keep you to it?
- What do you expect the hardest bit will be?
- What do you think the possible obstacles might be and how will you overcome them?
- What do you need to remember if things get difficult for you again?
- What will be the benefits for you that will make the effort worth it?
- Who is going to be able to help and who do you feel will be more part of the problem?
- How long do you think it will take before you feel this is not a big problem any longer?
- How will you remind yourself about the things you know help?

Figure 5.2   *Questions for ending and after-care*

Evaluating the counselling and planning ending

It is helpful to distinguish between treatment goals and life goals (Ticho 1972) otherwise counselling can become unduly prolonged. It is not a treatment goal to help a client find a partner or a job, for example, although the treatment goal might be to develop specific social skills in order to meet that goal. Counselling is the beginning of a process which does not demand that the counsellor be there at the end. Figure 5.2 lists a number of questions which focus on how the client could carry forward what she has gained or learnt from counselling.

Ending should always be on the agenda from the beginning. It should be our aim to remove ourselves from clients' lives as soon as possible; as soon as the clients are confident that they can carry on the changes they have begun to make. Otherwise there is the danger of dependency and loss of focus in the work. An agency which offers ongoing support to clients has to define it in such a way that it does not become confused with goal-directed counselling.

In SFT clients define the goals of counselling and largely determine when counselling should end. To some counsellors this will sound like a recipe for long-term counselling, but for most clients brief counselling is their treatment of choice. They have far less ambitious goals, often of quite a different character from the counsellor's, and are more satisfied with achieving limited, but realistic, goals than the counsellors often are. Scaling is a useful tool for describing endings. The counsellor asks the client what will be 'good enough' for her on a scale of zero to ten, with zero being the status quo and ten being the morning after a miracle. He then invites her to describe what will be happening or not happening when she has reached the desired point on the scale. Rarely do clients aspire to being a ten; the most common answers are seven or eight.

It is crucial that there is a clear agreement as to what will constitute the signs that the ending is near. Without such definition it is very difficult to monitor progress. Experience teaches us that endings are not always as clear cut as we would like and there can be a difference in perception between the counsellor and the client as to whether ending is appropriate. The solution-focused counsellor will always give the client the benefit of the doubt. In all forms of counselling, endings need preparation and sensitive handling. In brief therapy, when time has been an issue, badly handled endings can leave clients feeling that their problem has been trivialised, or that they have been written off as beyond help. This can feed into previous negative experiences and leave the client with a devastating sense of failure and rejection.

6

The Role of the Counsellor in SFT

The brief counsellor needs to believe in the validity of time-limited work and be able to communicate this to clients. In addition, he needs to have the capacity to form the therapeutic alliance quickly, be skilled in formulating goals with the client and be disciplined in keeping a focus on the central issue.

Figure 6.1 is useful in clarifying some of the differences between brief and long-term therapists. The figure oversimplifies the picture in so far as it gives the impression that brief counsellors do not believe that long-term counselling is ever appropriate, which would be an absurd position to occupy. Nor is it likely that any counsellor believes that counselling is 'almost always benign' and never harmful to clients. With particular reference to solution-focused counselling, the figure highlights:

1   The distinction between an assumption that there are always underlying issues to presenting problems and one which does not accept a hierarchical order or levels of problems in which one problem is constructed as 'deeper' or more 'real' than another. The solution-focused counsellor attends more to the context in which problems arise than to a structural or functional analysis of them.

2   The importance of the client working between the sessions. The sessions are only means to an end not an end in themselves. It is how the learning experienced there is translated into 'life' which makes the difference. In brief work it is necessary to make maximum use of the time available and that requires an active plan being implemented outside the counselling room.

3   The process by which a counsellor facilitates movement for change which will hopefully continue after the counselling has ended. All counsellors want this of course, but in

Long-term counsellor	Short-term counsellor
1 Seeks change in basic character	Prefers pragmatism, parsimony and least radical intervention; does not believe in the notion of 'cure'
2 Believes that significant change is unlikely in everyday life	Maintains an adult developmental perspective from which change is viewed as inevitable
3 Sees presenting problems as reflecting more basic pathology	Emphasises patient's strengths and resources
4 Wants to 'be there' as patient makes significant changes	Accepts that many changes will occur 'after counselling'
5 Sees counselling as having a 'timeless' quality	Does not accept the timelessness of some models of counselling
6 Unconsciously recognises the fiscal convenience of long-term patients	Fiscal issues often muted, either by the nature of the practice or the organisational structure
7 Views counselling as almost always benign and useful	Views counselling as sometimes useful and sometimes harmful
8 Sees counselling as being the most important part of the patient's life	Sees being in the world as more important than being in counselling
9 Views counsellor as responsible only for treating a given patient	Views counsellor as having responsibility for treatment of a population

Figure 6.1   *Comparative dominant values of the long-term and short-term counsellor (Budman and Gurman, 1992. Reprinted with permission)*

solution-focused therapy (SFT) there is a strong emphasis on minimal intervention whereby the counsellor only takes 'as many sessions as are needed, and not one more'. The essential task of the counsellor is to help the client to become aware of the number of choices available to her and to trust her to act wisely. SFT also takes the view that the counsellor is part of the problem-solution system and has an influence on whether the counselling becomes shortened or prolonged. There is ample research evidence for the efficacy of brief counselling (see Chapter 1) but there is still a credibility gap among those practitioners who underestimate the impact of brief interventions (Steenbarger 1994, Warner 1996). In the latter study, the underestimation was greatest for those clients seen for fewer sessions. Counsellors considered counselling to have been more helpful for those clients whom they had seen for more sessions, however this was not borne out by the clients' reports.

Counsellor skills and qualities

The counsellor needs to communicate with the client in clear and comprehensible terms. In order to achieve clarity the counsellor matches the client's language and imagery, provided that the language chosen does not trap the client in her problem situation. The counsellor needs discipline in order to ask solution-oriented questions without being side-tracked into irrelevant (for this model) culs-de-sac. This is one of the most difficult challenges for an inexperienced solution-focused counsellor.

The counsellor needs patience, tenacity, warmth, tact and curiosity in order to enter the client's frame of reference in a respectful, non-intrusive manner. A relentless form of questioning, such as in a search for exceptions to the problem, can make the client feel pressurised into giving the counsellor the kind of answer she thinks he wants. The skilled counsellor will break the question-answer cycle by making empathic and reflective statements. Nylund and Corsiglia (1994: 10) speculate that:

> A therapist who learns the solution-oriented approach without receiving sufficient training in the relational and emotional aspects of therapy is likely to engage in solution 'forced' therapy by asking a barrage of questions. In particular, if a trainee does not learn pacing, attending to the client's non verbal responses and body language, then the solution-forced phenomenon may grow rapidly.

Sensitivity to the dynamics of the relationship requires that the counsellor notices and responds appropriately to the body language of the client, otherwise the client will withdraw co-operation. SFT is a way of being 'present with' the client. There are times when any counsellor feels lost and unsure how to proceed; at such times the golden rule in SFT is to ask the client. If the counsellor is doubtful whether what he is doing is helpful or is unclear in which direction to move, he needs to trust the client enough to consult and find out. An inexperienced solution-focused counsellor lacking confidence in his own competence, will find it more difficult to show such vulnerability than will an experienced worker who is at ease with the fact that the more he knows the more he realises what he doesn't know.

In brief counselling it is important for the counsellor to form a therapeutic alliance as early as possible. It is crucial that the client feels safe and accepted by the counsellor. A feeling of blame, judgement or disapproval is incompatible with the principles of solution-focused working. Although transference, as used by psychodynamic counsellors, is not a central feature of SFT, the counsellor should attend to what is happening in the room and if appropriate feed back his perceptions to the client. In order for brief counselling to be effective it is helpful if the client experiences positive transference towards the counsellor. The counsellor may consciously model ways of approaching problems by sharing therapeutic stories with the client; he may also use the feelings engendered by the client as clues which point towards solutions. Although the emotional temperature in SFT interviews tends to be low, since ventilation of feelings is not in itself considered essential for effective counselling, this does not mean that the counsellor devalues or ignores feelings.

The counsellor needs the skill to sense when to move between problem and solution talk. Kiser, Piercy and Lipchik (1993: 235) state: 'The movement in SFT from problems to solutions is not automatic. It involves considerable therapeutic skill to help a client move from feeling bad and talking about negative experiences to feeling bad and shifting focus to more positive emotions.' Clients vary a great deal in the balance they strike between their focus on the problem and their hopes for the future. The counsellor paces himself to meet the needs of each client. Clients of solution-focused counselling often report feeling tired at the end of sessions and there is no doubt that they have to work very hard, mentally and emotionally.

The counsellor has to be able to work without feeling that he needs to know a lot about the problem. This is not always easy for someone trained in other therapies. In some respects it is easier for counsellors to like or respect their clients when the conversation is at least as much about solutions as it is problems. There can be a sense of a downward spiral when sessions become preoccupied by the minute details of problems. This is hardly surprising, as there comes a point when for some clients talking about their depression, for example, can only leave them feeling worse not better.

In SFT, the task of the counsellor is not to uncover the lost 'truth' which will explain the client's current problems – the 'counsellor as psychological detective' model – but to create a climate in which people have a voice to express their experience and have their strengths and competence affirmed. This is often denied those whose view of the world has been devalued, dismissed or suppressed – for example, people with disabilities. By focusing upon interactions, 'the journey outwards', rather than upon intra-psychic phenomena, 'the journey inwards', solution-focused counselling acknowledges these perspectives as having legitimacy in a public context. Counselling becomes an exercise in generating alternative attitudes, interpretations, choices and strategies.

The counsellor needs good powers of concentration and memory and an ability to give the client succinct, balanced summaries of exceptions and successes. It can be helpful to take notes during the sessions. Without notes, it is difficult to remember answers to the miracle or scaling questions. Taking notes of solution talk and exceptions to the problem also reinforces the importance of these steps towards solutions.

In one of the few published studies of process in SFT, Metcalf and Thomas (1994) observed couples receiving SFT at the Brief Family Therapy Center in Milwaukee. They found that clients had a very different perception of the counsellor's role to that of the counsellor. The clients described counsellors as guides, saviours, mediators, friends and outsiders. They described the work of the counsellor as 'making suggestions, saying what would work, being a sounding board'. These were not the terms chosen by the counsellors to describe what they had done. They preferred to see themselves as being 'a consultant, a listener, as someone who gave ideas, highlighted competencies and looked for strengths and resources'. Clients tended to give the counsellor credit for success, whereas an important principle of SFT is to give clients the credit for their progress. The clients also described their problems very differently from the way in which the counsellor described them. The study showed that the counsellors were more active and directive and used more pathological language than the literature advocates. This study suggests that solution-focused counsellors are as likely as any other type of counsellor to be perceived by clients as acting out of character with the model they espouse. In another study, Gale and Newfield (1992), analysed a marital counselling session conducted by a leading practitioner of SFT, Bill O'Hanlon, in order to identify precisely what the counsellor did. They identified nine categories of characteristic counsellor response. These were:

1   pursuing a response over many turns in the conversation
2   clarifying unclear references
3   modifying assertions until he receives the response he is seeking
4   posing questions or possible problems and answering these questions himself
5   overlapping his talk with the husband or wife's in order to get a turn in the conversation
6   reformulating problems
7   offering a possible answer to a question
8   using humour to change a topic from a problematic theme to a solution theme
9   ignoring the recipient's misunderstanding or rejection and continuing as if his assertion was accepted.

In this interview, the counsellor took on an expert role and steered the clients in the direction he believed to be helpful. He often talked over clients and on occasions put words into their mouths in ways which observers might construe as manipulative. These comments may sound critical of the counsellor, but those who have heard and watched Bill O'Hanlon working (including myself) hold him in high regard as a creative and skilled practitioner. Some of the ways in which he sought to influence clients were none the less inconsistent with the principles and techniques of SFT. A similar criticism could be made of most practitioners that they do not practice what they preach. It is perhaps encouraging to know that there is no one right way of using a particular model of counselling and that the model inevitably changes in various respects depending on the temperament of the person using it.

CASE EXAMPLE

The following case conveys the flavour of a typical piece of SFT.

The client was a white female in her forties, married, with three children. She had a well-paid 'white-collar' job in which she had to work long hours while juggling childcare and responsibilities for an elderly mother. Her husband often worked away from home. Approximately two years prior to coming for counselling, she had felt 'on the verge of a nervous breakdown' and had to take time off work. She had returned to work after three months and had renegotiated a less stressful role in the organisation. However, she had again begun to experience similar stress-related symptoms and immediately prior to presenting for counselling had taken sick leave. She described herself as being anxious, indecisive and short tempered at home, particularly with the children. Her memory and concentration were poor and she was not sleeping well.

During the first session the client talked at length about her problems at home and at work, although she said she had felt unsure about doing so. The counsellor validated the client's feelings and experiences, while listening for examples of coping strategies. He asked the miracle question and received an answer which included:

• sleeping better
• feeling mentally calmer
• being more supported by her husband
• playing with her children and not shouting at them
• being back at work and coping with the pressures without being snappy and making mistakes.

The counsellor asked, 'On a scale of zero to ten, ten representing the morning after the miracle and zero the worst you've ever been, where would you put yourself today? The client answered that she was at three. At the end of the session the counsellor invited the client to notice times when she managed to control her worry habit even a little and remember what she did to achieve that. She was also asked to write down a list of things which she thought she could do in order to reduce her stress levels. The client appeared motivated and keen to use the time off work to 'sort herself out'.

When she returned for the second session, the counsellor asked, 'What's better?' She described situations when she felt free from stress – gardening, going out with her friend to an evening class, reading, taking her children to the cinema. The feedback given by the counsellor congratulated her on what she had managed to do. In terms of utilising her skills and experience, the counsellor noted that she had a lot of energy and was creative and caring in her approach to the problem. The counsellor reminded her that she had overcome this problem before and wondered whether she could remember anything which had worked the last time. She felt that her husband had been very supportive then and that she needed him to support her more at the moment.

During the third session the client reported that she was surprised (as was her husband) at how well she was doing.

> *Client*: I've been able to think about going back to work without it waking me up in the middle of the night.
> *Counsellor*: How did you manage to do that?
> *Client*: I think I've come to see that there's more to life than just working all the time. I've begun to stand back from it.

The client had begun to change her 'viewing' of her problem. The counsellor invited her to continue doing what was working and to think through the implications of her new way of looking at her job.

At the fourth session she reported that she found scaling helpful and used it each day to measure how she had dealt with particularly stressful situations. She felt calmer, more relaxed and had stopped 'flying' at her daughter. She was experimenting with taking small manageable steps towards controlling her anxiety.

She reported that she was six on the scale. She was sleeping better and had come to realise that things would never be perfect. She would be happy to achieve a seven, not a ten. The counsellor affirmed the client's self-awareness and problem-solving strategies, and reinforced her repertoire by expressing the view that, once acquired, these skills would not be lost, as long as they were consolidated by regular practice. The counsellor also suggested that skills used in the domestic arena were transferable to the work environment. This belief helped to increase the possibility that the counselling could be effective and brief.

> *Counsellor*: I've seen you make progress and there's every reason to think that you can maintain that. I think people can transfer these skills. I think it's important to realise it's basically the same stuff. It's just a different place or environment. You've got the tools there. You're doing the job already.

By the sixth session the client felt she was handling relationships at home much better, but felt anxious about the impending return to work. Despite her apprehension, she had developed a 'survival plan' for her first few weeks back. Her solutions included a determination to say no to extra work, a request for a meeting with her boss to get more resources and avoidance of any unnecessary travel. The feedback to the client complimented the client on her self-care skills and her courage in facing up to a stressful situation. The client wanted reassurance that the counselling could continue for a few more weeks until she felt more confident about work.

In the next session the client said that she felt that she had had a setback and that she felt quite depressed about work again. She had visited her workplace but had felt quite overwhelmed and her colleagues had not been very friendly. The counsellor reassured her that 'practising new habits is often bumpy'. He also explored how she was managing to stop things getting worse. Her answer was the increased support at home.

In the final two sessions the client revisited the miracle question and applied it to her work situation – for example, how colleagues would be treating her, the amount and kind of work she would be doing. She recognised that she had 'moved down a gear' and was more in control. She liked her 'new self'. After nine sessions she felt that she had learnt sound strategies for handling her stress. She decided to end counselling. At the end of the counselling she offered the following comments:

> I've noticed that everything seems to be looking forwards. It seems to be a lot more realistic. You don't waste a lot of time. It's not just a case of someone listening to you, it's doing something about it, and what I've noticed is that in a conversation you've said to me, 'How was your week? How did you rate your week?' Now I know next week you'll probably ask me the same question, so you make me really accountable. I feel as though I'm sitting here talking about how my week's been, then suddenly you'll sort of pull it forward. The first time it took my breath away. I felt after it a great sense of achievement. This is a good way to go. This is a nice way.

The above case typifies many of the characteristics of a solution-focused interview:

1   The counsellor works collaboratively within the client's frame of reference and utilises her motivation, energy and imagination.

2   The counsellor supports the client's choices and experiments as she works towards her goals.

3   The counsellor identifies and trusts the client's strengths.

4   The counsellor seeks exceptions and uses the miracle question and scaling to measure progress.

5   The counsellor mines the past to discover the client's resources and transferable skills.

6   The future orientation is much more to the fore than the past. While not wishing to raise unrealistic expectations, counsellors need to be people of hope who believe that change can and does take place; at the same time the counsellor needs to realise that it is very difficult for many people to take an optimistic view of the future, given their experience to date. People can be stronger because of their painful past, but they can also feel dispirited, beaten and exhausted.

7   The counsellor openly compliments the client on those things she is doing which are helpful. It is empowering for clients to be given credit for success, particularly if they see themselves as being inadequate or out of control. However, it is not always easy for people to accept and own their achievements and there is little to be gained by the counsellor trying to persuade clients that they have achieved more than they are willing to own. Clients may be anxious that help will be withdrawn if they acknowledge that they are coping better.

8   The counselling ends when the client is confident that she can maintain progress. This does not preclude the natural anxiety on both sides which can accompany endings. The counsellor will leave the door open for the client to return if necessary.

9   The client has become her own counsellor. Talmon (1996) talks about the counsellor being like a singing teacher who sings along with a pupil to help her to sing in tune, but who then stops to let the singer hear her own voice. The structure of our craniums and voice equipment is such that the singer hears a different sound from that heard by the person who is listening. O'Hanlon (1995) uses the analogy of a curling player whose partner sweeps the ice in front of the puck in order to smooth its path and help it to keep moving in the direction which the player wants.

Counsellor interventions

In an analysis of four transcripts of solution-focused interviews, B. O'Connell (1997) identified specific categories of counsellor interventions. Many of these related to rapport-building strategies such as:

- encouragement
- support giving
- agreement prompts
- joint completion of client sentences
- use of humour
- validation of client's experiences
- normalisation statements.

Empathy in the interviews focused on those actions which the client was already using in order to deal with the problem. This functional empathy was congruent with the action orientation in SFT which affirms that the client is already doing things which are helpful. The 'getting alongside' approach was a conscious strategy to build a co-operative, collaborative relationship. Rapport building helped to motivate clients towards solutions and took place throughout, even when the main focus had shifted to strategies and action plans.

Joint completion of clients' sentences was a deliberate therapeutic strategy (Gale and Newfield 1992), designed to increase trust with the client by demonstrating the accuracy and empathy of the counsellor's listening and understanding.

Other interventions were more clearly related to exploring the themes of change, solution and strategy:

1 change talk
2 solution talk
3 strategy talk.

Change talk
In change talk a key theme is 'seeking difference'. When the clients talked about problem or solution events, the counsellor attempted to find, in Bateson's phrase, 'the difference that makes the difference' (1972). The counsellor used circular questions to discover the impact which an event had upon the clients and other significant people. The ability to notice difference in the

problem situation injected fluidity and dynamism into what otherwise felt to the client like a fixed and rigid pattern.

Solution talk

The focus of solution talk was to construct the future which the client wanted. The counsellor used presuppositional questions, the principal of which was the miracle question.

EXAMPLE

> *Counsellor*: Let me ask you a question Tom we often ask people. It's a bit of a strange question but people often find it very helpful. If you woke up tomorrow and somehow things had got better, what would be the first things you would notice?
>
> *Client*: I think if I woke up and felt like I did twenty years ago, then I'd feel that must have been a miracle.
>
> *Counsellor*: So, what would be different for you that day?
>
> *Client*: Life would be a lot slower. I think life is too fast anyway, but with me I make it even faster.
>
> *Counsellor*: So what would you be doing more slowly after the miracle?
>
> *Client*: I'd get up at the right time to go to the day centre. At the moment I get up too early and worry about getting there when I don't need to. It's part of my anxiety. I worry about everything.
>
> *Counsellor*: So if a miracle happened, you wouldn't be worried about so many things.
>
> *Client*: No. I'd have a clear mind, I'd be remembering things better and my concentration would be better.
>
> *Counsellor*: What else would be different for you?
>
> *Client*: I'd be able to relax more. I'd be able to plan ahead, maybe what I want to do tomorrow or next week. Then think to myself I've to go all out and do it. Whereas now I say I'm going to do things but I don't bother to do them. I think if the miracle happened I'd try to look on the positive side of things. At the moment I look very much on the negative side. I'd start enjoying life.
>
> *Counsellor*: And that's something you'd very much like.
>
> *Client*: Yes. I've always enjoyed mixing with people. I go to the club on Tuesdays, the people are great. I can laugh and joke if I'm not feeling too bad. I leave there and as soon as I get back to the house I'm a different person. When I'm in company I'm a different person.
>
> *Counsellor*: So after the miracle will you be spending more time with other people or more time on your own?
>
> *Client*: I'd sooner be among other people, but not big crowds, I couldn't stick that. If I had a good social life, going back to my house each day, I could relax. I'm sure I could. I could watch the box and have a good night's sleep. I think I'd be 95 per cent there, I'm sure I would.

Strategy talk
Strategy talk was conversation which related to what the client was already doing or was planning to do about managing the problem. It took place more towards the end of interviews than at the beginning, but was present throughout. Forms of strategy talk included:

- *Coping questions* Here the counsellor elicited from the client how he had managed to cope, despite all the difficulties. On other occasions the counsellor recognised that the client was already working on problem-solving strategies and facilitated him in extending his repertoire.
- *Multiple-choice questions* When exploring strategies, on occasions the counsellor asked the client multiple-choice questions about available strategies. In this example the counsellor pre-empted unhelpful strategies, while at the same time suggesting that the client had, or might have, found other ways of tackling the problem.

    Counsellor: So what do you do? Do you jump up and go into total panic or go and do fifty things about it? Do you talk to someone? Or do you deal with it differently?
    Client: Well, I mean there's two ways I've found that I . . .

This may be interpreted by the client as suggestion making, but to the counsellor it is more a stimulus to promote client choice.

- *Scaling questions* These were used to measure confidence, motivation and progress and are described more fully in Chapter 4.

The solution-focused therapist does have a structure in mind when working with clients. De Shazer and Berg (1997) identified the marks of the true solution-focused session as being:

1 At some point in the first interview, the therapist will ask the miracle question.
2 At least once during the first interview and at subsequent ones, the client will be asked to rate something on a scale of zero to ten.
3 At some point during the interview, the therapist will take a break.

4   After this intermission, the therapist will compliment the client. This will frequently be followed by a suggestion or a homework task (an 'experiment').

This structure is perhaps too mechanical and prescriptive. I would prefer to give the therapist more discretion and flexibility than the above sequence seems to allow. Some clients need time and space to express their distress and it can be counterproductive and disrespectful to move them on too quickly without acknowledging their pain and concerns. We do not want to encourage a form of counselling by numbers which could be delivered via a computer.

7

Solution-Focused Supervision

Inskipp (1996) argues that supervision is becoming established as a discipline in its own right, with its own emerging models and skills. It is not simply a mirror reflection of therapy models. Good supervision in any tradition will tend to have similar positive qualities. In describing the characteristics of solution-focused supervision, it is not my intention to claim that these are by any means exclusive to the model.

The family therapy tradition of co-working and live supervision by members of a therapeutic team means that therapists learn 'on the job' by taking on various roles within the team (Merl 1995). Instant feedback from colleagues highlights the multi-faceted view of a session and tends to expose individual bias or prejudice. This supportive learning which, on occasions, may include the client, reduces the need for one-to-one supervision. It is this open, live, team approach which explains the apparent lack of interest shown by leading solution-focused therapists, such as Steve de Shazer, in one-to-one supervision. However, not all solution-focused therapists belong to teams.

Building on competence

Solution-focused supervision validates the competence and resources of the supervisee, emphasises the importance of clear incremental goals and identifies pre-existing solutions and exceptions to problems in the supervisee's work. It focuses more on what the supervisee is doing, rather than on client issues directly. It attends to process from an interactional perspective rather than from an intra-psychic one.

In solution-focused supervision the supervisor regards the supervisee as competent, skilled and co-operative. Wetchler (1990) describes the role of the supervisor as concentrating on what the supervisee is doing effectively, and assisting her to continue to do those things. By affirming and extending competence, the supervisor is helping to lay the foundations for professional identity and continuing professional development. In solution-focused supervision there is a clear contract which identifies learning goals for the supervisee based on her current level of professional development (Selekman and Todd 1995).

In my experience as a supervisor, many therapists tend to be hard on themselves, to underestimate their competence and disown their skills. Good supervision will counter this by providing clear and constructive criticism in an appropriate blend of support and challenge.

Supervisors, who are likely to have clearer theoretical awareness and greater technical expertise than most other therapists, occupy a powerful role as gatekeepers to the profession. Their role however is to develop the unique talents of their supervisees, not to produce carbon copies of themselves. This requires a respect for difference and a trust in the choices supervisees make, even if on occasions they do not entirely coincide with the views of the supervisor.

Try something different

If supervision, in the opinion of either party, is not working, the parties adopt a non-defensive, pragmatic attitude towards change, based on the solution-focused principle that 'if something is not working try something different'. This requires flexibility, a willingness to experiment and a constant discipline in evaluation. The supervisor aims to create a climate in which change is the norm and the supervisory relationship itself is reviewable. Given human nature and professional sensitivities, such an ideal is not always met! Although the effectiveness of the relationship is open to review, transference and countertransference issues are not normally addressed as fully as may be the case in other models.

No problem remains constant, it is always evolving. Supervisors regard supervisees as capable of change. They are not surprised at the ability of therapists to change their interventions with clients, in fact they expect and encourage it. This expectation may increase the possibility that change will happen. Openness and flexibility in choosing the best way to work with any particular client have become the norm for most therapists and solution-focused methods reflect this pragmatism.

Supporting expertise

A solution-focused approach tends to emphasise the more collegial aspects of the supervisory relationship. Thomas (1994) describes the supervisor as 'coaxing the expertise' out of the supervisee, rather than being a dispenser of wisdom. The supervisor fosters an atmosphere of mutual respect in which both parties celebrate skills, creative ideas, personal qualities and therapeutic successes. Supervision is an 'inventive art' (Cantwell and Holmes 1995). Curiosity, an attitude encouraged in solution-focused therapy (SFT), prompts the supervisor to find out how best to co-operate uniquely with this supervisee. This exploration may cover the supervisee's own preferred learning styles, use of language, prior experience of effective and ineffective supervision, stage of professional development and personal qualities and circumstances.

Supervision is essentially a collaborative partnership in which both sides take responsibility for negotiating the goals and options available. In practice, the balance of collaboration will vary according to the level of expertise and experience of the supervisee.

The 'one down' position

The supervisor, while conscious of the ethical and professional responsibilities of the role, adopts a 'one down' position in order to learn from the supervisee how to act as supervisor. The supervisor, in Cantwell and Holmes's (1995) phrase, 'leads from one step behind'. In practice, this means that the supervisor does not assume the role of expert in all matters, but seeks to validate expertise in the supervisee. Contrary to critical opinion, solution-focused methods do not pressurise the client or the supervisee, but instead employ creative, reflective silences in which both parties can explore possible ways forward. Such encounters develop a respectful partnership in which the central role of the therapist receives full recognition. The 'one down' position also helps to reduce the chances of unintentional oppressive practice, which is always possible given the range of differences potentially present between supervisor and supervisee: age, gender, race, class, beliefs, sexual preference and disability. This egalitarianism does not of course remove from the supervisor the obligation to confront an incompetent therapist or one whose personal issues are interfering with therapeutic processes.

From a constructivist standpoint, supervision is a mutual social construction in which the meaning of language is negotiated within a specific context (Anderson and Swim 1995). There is an understanding that there is no 'one truth' about either the therapy itself, or indeed about the supervision. There are multiple realities, voices to be heard, contexts to be respected. The supervisor will draw the worker's attention to the way she uses language to describe realities 'out there' as if they had independent objectivity. This sensitivity towards language can help to make the supervisee think carefully about the ways in which she shapes the client's problem and deals with it. It can also open up rich possibilities for understanding the many meanings which clients attach to events in their lives.

Supervision can be seen as a 'parallel process' to therapy itself, though not to be confused with it. If, for example, a therapist is having a problem in helping to move a client forward, the supervisor might use a number of interventions which are also used in therapy, such as the miracle question, to help the supervisee make progress. Supervision is therefore a form of reflective experiential learning for the supervisee.

This solution-focused template will include values, attitudes, expectations and techniques. The techniques will include exception seeking, giving credit to the supervisee, the miracle question and scaling.

Exception seeking

In this example, the supervisee had succeeded in gaining the confidence of an initially suspicious and cautious client.

> *Supervisee*: It was very hard going for the first few weeks. There were long silences which didn't feel very productive. I felt as if she was testing me out. When I started to offer suggestions, she always had some reason why she couldn't do anything.
> *Supervisor*: You mean things got a bit easier after the first few sessions? How did that come about?

Supervisee: I stopped making suggestions, so I felt less frustrated. I told her that many people would not have coped as well as she had done. I began to compliment her on the way she was thinking about the problem and said that she would know when to do something about it.

Supervisor: It sounds as if once you made less demands on her and took a more positive view, you began to get on better with her.

Supervisee: It was really strange how the less I tried to push, the more she seemed to come out of her shell. I think she was amazed at me complimenting her.

Supervisor: Your approach seems to have opened a few doors for her. Some therapists might have been tempted to batter the door down, but you seemed to sense it was better to back off and give her some space. Is that something you intend to continue with or even do more of?

The supervisor invites the supervisee to recall those times when, as the therapist, she managed, if only temporarily, to do something different with the client which worked. Exception seeking follows the SFT principle of finding solutions more in solution than in problem talk. Rather than analysing why things may have felt stuck (which could lead to a long speculative exploration), the supervisor helps the supervisee to reflect on those exceptions when the stuckness was not there, or not there to the same degree.

• What was happening on those occasions? Who said what? How?
• What made the difference? How did it make a difference?
• Could this be developed?

In the above example the therapist had learnt to give the client space and genuine positive feedback. This was the key which opened the door for the client.

Giving credit to the supervisee

Therapists need to have their own therapeutic skills validated and due credit given for good practice, just as they in turn give clients credit for their successes. They need to know what they did well and how they did it, in order to be able to reproduce it. Solution-focused supervision sessions are likely to begin with the question: 'What did you feel you succeeded in doing with this particular client?' (Merl 1995). Identifying competence is more likely to increase professional confidence than a preoccupation with deficits and mistakes. If supervisees can come to believe that they are basically competent they are more likely to be receptive to new learning and more willing to experiment in their practice. They may also accept that mistakes are permissible and present opportunities for valuable learning. Therapists who are clear about their strengths and their limitations are more likely to work within their competence as stated in professional Codes of Ethics and Practice.

The miracle question

The supervisor may use the miracle question, 'If you were working better with this client and your current difficulties had been overcome, what would be the first signs for you that a miracle had happened?'

> *Supervisee*: My heart wouldn't sink when I saw him in the waiting room.
> *Supervisor*: After the miracle how would you be feeling and what would you be thinking when you saw him there?
> *Supervisee*: I would smile at him the way I do with most clients and sound a bit more enthusiastic in asking him to come in.
> *Supervisor*: What else?
> *Supervisee*: When he starts talking he would let me get a word in edgeways, rather than just launching into the verbal attack he usually does.
> *Supervisor*: What difference would that make to you?
> *Supervisee*: I'd feel I had something to offer rather than just being a dumping ground for all his complaints, without him being willing to let me help him change.
> *Supervisor*: What else would be happening once the miracle has happened?
> *Supervisee*: I wouldn't be feeling so weary and hopeless after seeing him.
> *Supervisor*: How would you be feeling at the end of a session?
> *Supervisee*: I would feel that he had worked harder than me and that it was worth while trying to help him.
> *Supervisor*: If we were having supervision on this client three months from now and you were telling me things were much better how would it have come about? What would have happened to have made it happen?
> *Supervisee*: I would have found ways of keeping him on the subject and listening to what I have to say for a change.
> *Supervisor*: I wonder how you will have managed to do that?
> *Supervisee*: I would have an agreed agenda for a session and interrupt him once he goes off on a tangent. I also think I would give him

things to do between sessions and start off a session by asking him whether he's done them or not. I think if I could get him to keep to the point most of the time I wouldn't mind if occasionally he went off on a monologue.

Supervisor: So you would have more of a structure to the session than you have at the moment?

Supervisee: I think I would have limited the sessions to less than an hour as well. Then I wouldn't feel so drained at the end of them. I think I could do a better job with him in half an hour rather than an hour.

Supervisor: That sounds as if you are thinking of ways which will help you to be more effective and to look after yourself at the same time. How will you have done this without your client feeling you are rejecting him or can't handle him?

The miracle question encourages supervisees to talk about improving their practice without feeling that they have to defend or justify themselves. The future orientation reduces the possibility of them feeling discouraged or de-skilled by past failures. As long as the supervisor moves at the right pace, the miracle question should not raise unrealistic expectations, but should relate closely to the supervisees' current level of expertise.

Scaling

Scaling is often used in solution-focused supervision to develop answers to the miracle question, but it can also be used at other points.

Supervisor: On a scale of zero to ten, ten being your effectiveness with this client after the miracle and zero the lowest it's ever been, where would you say you are today?
Where would you like to get to?
What would it look like when you got there?
What would be happening that's not happening at the moment?
What would have stopped happening?
What would need to happen for that to happen?
What would be the first thing you would do?
What would the client notice was different?
What would you need to remind yourself about?
If there were setbacks how would you get back on track?

The supervisor may ask scaling questions in relation to the supervisee's confidence or motivation to work more effectively with this client.

Supervisor: On a scale of zero to ten, zero being the lowest you can get and ten being the highest, how confident are you that you can improve your work with this client?
Is that good enough for you to make a start?
If not, where would you need to get to for that to happen?
What would be the first step for you to build up your confidence?
What would your client notice was different about you?

In terms of motivation to change, the supervisor uses the same scale and follows it up with supplementary questions.

Is that motivation high enough for you to make a start?
If not, where do you need to get to?
How could you move one point on the motivation scale?
How would the client experience your new motivation?
If things were to improve with this client, how would it affect your work with other clients?
How would it affect your level of job satisfaction?

There is a legitimate place for the supervisor to encourage and compliment the therapist on what he is doing well. The restorative function of supervision is very important (Inskipp and Proctor 1989). Supervision should recharge the batteries and stimulate the brain cells.

Goals

Solution-focused work stresses the importance of negotiating a clear picture of specific outcomes to result from therapy. Both parties monitor whether clear and realistic goals are being set with the client and whether progress is being made towards achieving them. Therapy is a purposeful activity to be pursued in such a way that it does not last any longer than is necessary for the client to move significantly towards the agreed goals. Perhaps one of the most useful ways in which a solution-focused approach can help supervisees is in the focus on endings. As a model of brief therapy, it aims to have a clear sight of the ending from the beginning wherever possible. This decreases the chances of work finishing abruptly or drifting. Using a scaling question, for example, might reveal that the client expects the therapy to finish when he or she moves from two to five. Supervision can focus on how the therapist could monitor this progress, recognise the signs along the way and stop when the goal has been reached.

To summarise, solution-focused supervision is a respectful and creative activity which uses many of the interventions used in the therapy itself. It is competence-based and future-oriented. It stays close to the supervisee's agenda without sacrificing the ethical and professional responsibilities of the supervisor.

8

Questions Frequently Asked About SFT

Participants at workshops often display an open-mindedness about requiring new skills. At the same time, some have reservations about aspects of the model and seek clarification about what they feel are its deficiencies. In this chapter I would like to address those concerns, not in order to act as an apologist for solution-focused therapy (SFT), but to acknowledge difference and to attempt to clarify misunderstandings.

Objections to SFT

1 Is it the case that the method largely ignores people's feelings and concentrates on behaviour?
Different therapies have different ways of explaining the interconnectedness of cognitions, emotions and behaviour. Does thinking differently make the person feel differently and consequently act differently? Or does the person need to feel differently, then think differently, then act differently? Or act differently, then feel and think differently? Some clearly give priority to one element over others, while others seek to include all equally and regard therapies which do not do so as inherently defective. Effective counselling addresses the holistic needs of people, including their emotional lives. Failure to do so is likely to lead to the client terminating the relationship. Our feelings influence our thinking, our decisions and our actions. Expressing powerful feelings can be a catalyst for change. Solution-focused practitioners initiate and support client expression of feelings, not because they believe that catharsis is in itself necessarily therapeutic, or the essence of counselling for all clients, but because feelings are an integral part of people's unique experience and that whole experience must be respected and validated. Each client has different needs, with some needing to ventilate emotions more

than others. The effective counsellor is flexible in responding to those needs. In brief counselling the more focused nature of the work precludes the wide-ranging emotional exploration which is possible in long-term counselling. It is probably true, although no research has been done on this, that the amount of time spent directly exploring feelings in SFT is less than in many other models, especially in those which focus primarily on feelings. De Shazer and Berg (1992), however, argue that helping the client to change the meaning of her experience automatically brings about a change in feelings about the problem. SFT tends to share the outlook of strategic counsellors (Kleckner, Frank, Bland, Amendt and DuRee Bryant 1992), who do not attempt to change people's feelings directly but who suggest that clients' feelings may catch up with changes in their attitudes or behaviours. Clients do not need to wait until they feel better before they begin to change things in their lives.

Fear of failure and ambivalence about change can affect people's willingness and ability to discover exceptions to the problem or to answer the miracle question. With some clients it is important to address first the ambivalence which they feel about change. Others are unsure about any type of forward-planning. Counsellor recognition of these feelings is a form of joining the client where she is and ensuring that any future interventions genuinely fit the clients.

At all stages SFT validates and acknowledges people's feelings. Feeling-oriented questions and statements appear in pre-session change enquiries, exception seeking, answers to the miracle questions, scaling, goal setting and discussions about client competence and coping strategies. Linking client feelings, thoughts and behaviours strengthens the therapeutic bond and facilitates change.

Congruence, warmth, empathy and non-possessiveness, the keys to effective counselling, are likely to thrive in the co-operative and respectful climate advocated in SFT.

2   Does SFT work or is it popular merely because it is brief and therefore economical?

There are of course many forms of brief counselling (see Chapter 1) and this objection could apply to them all. As far as SFT is concerned, although in practice it tends to be brief, there is no reason *per se* why this should be the case. Even clients who state a preference for short-term work may unearth issues which require long-term therapy. Some of SFT's characteristics – such as staying close to the client's view of the problem, using what the client brings, setting attainable goals and refraining from a search for causes – are more likely to lead to the counselling being brief than long term. At the same time, there are clients with whom one would use a solution-focused approach long term.

Brief counsellors are conscious of the need to structure time in such a way that it becomes an ally not an enemy. Being aware that the first session is often the last, whatever the preference of the therapist, imposes a responsibility on the therapist to make every session valuable and meaningful in its own right. Time becomes an enemy when a goal-driven approach demands a premature formulation of objectives accompanied by pressure towards a speedy resolution of the problem. This invariably results in bad counselling, whatever it is called. It can undermine the development of the trusting and safe relationship needed for clients to show openness and vulnerability. A wiser and more respectful therapeutic motto would be, *'festina lente* – hurry slowly'.

In addition to de Shazer's own research into the work at the Brief Family Therapy Center (see Chapter 1), Kiser (1988) and De Jong and Hopwood's (1996) studies of the BFTC broadly confirm that:

- More than three-quarters of clients fully met their treatment goals or made progress towards them.
- The average number of sessions was 3.0.
- The counselling was equally effective with a diversity of clients and did not vary according to the client–counsellor gender or racial mix.
- The same therapeutic procedures were effective across a wide range of client-identified problems.

McDonald (1994) researched the patients of a psychiatric outpatient department in which all the counsellors had received solution-focused training. In a follow-up study one year after treatment, a positive outcome was self-reported in 70 per cent of patients (71 per cent by their general practitioners), while 10 per cent of patients reported a negative outcome. There was a significant correlation between positive outcome and the length of treatment. The mean number of sessions for the improved group was 5.47 and for the unimproved 3.71. Long-standing problems did slightly less well. Those in the group which deteriorated were younger and all were female. Social class was not a factor, perhaps suggesting that brief therapy is accessible to a wide range of people and may be effective for those groups thought to be apprehensive of traditional forms of therapy.

Zimmerman, Prest and Wetzel (1997) compared the effects of a six-week solution-focused couples therapy group with a comparable no-treatment group. Although there was no significant difference between the groups on a measure of the couples' likelihood of divorce, there were significant improvements in a variety of areas, such as expression of affection and overall satisfaction with the relationship. There is anecdotal evidence that the model brings about change in clients, but limited published research which has been submitted to the academic community for scrutiny. The development of an active Europe-wide SFT research group will hopefully remedy this deficiency.

3   Is SFT only suitable for those clients who can identify specific issues on which they want to work, and not for clients with vague, chronic or severe mental health problems?

The implication behind this statement is that SFT is useful in 'easy' cases, but not in more demanding ones. As mentioned in Chapter 3, the model has been used and well documented in challenging settings with complex and difficult family, couple and individual problems.

Most clients come for counselling with a tangled web of conflicting emotions, thoughts, hopes and expectations. Many clients echo the sentiments of the serenity prayer: 'Give me the serenity to accept the things I cannot change, the courage to change the things I can and the wisdom to know the difference.' Knowing what to place in the 'change' box and what in the 'acceptance/serenity' box (M.F. O'Connell 1997) is not always easy.

The prevailing view among SFT practitioners is that no category of problem or 'type' of client should, a priori, be considered as unsuitable for this approach. This reflects the constructionist view of how problems become attached to people and how this in turn affects the way in which professionals treat them. Mental health workers report that many clients with chronic problems experience SFT as being quite different from other therapies which they have received and that this very novelty can help to break long-standing 'stuck' problem patterns. Every client experiences the 'problem' in a unique way. The counsellor who has read about the issues and problems which their clients commonly present – for example, processes in bereavement/eating disorders/substance abuse etc. – may access their clients' experiences more easily, provided that they respect the uniqueness of perceptions, resources, feelings and strategies which they bring.

The client may bring abilities which make the task easier for the counsellor, such as:

- being open to defining the problem as solvable
- identifying what she wants to change
- recalling deliberate exceptions to the problem
- being willing to imagine a different future
- feeling committed to experimenting with new behaviour
- being able to own genuine compliments
- feeling motivated to change.

Without such abilities, counselling will probably be slower and more uncertain in its outcome. It takes time for people to move from being a visitor or a complainant to being a customer. The counsellor will need to work harder to circumvent the negative forces which hold the person back from changing. This can be particularly challenging when the client is an involuntary client, sent by someone else; or when the resolution of the problem appears to be in the power and control of an absent third party.

Involuntary clients Many clients are sent for therapy because someone else thinks it is a good idea. That person often has power over them and wants to see changes result from the therapy. All therapists know the frustrations involved in trying to gain the co-operation of such clients. It is a mistake to expect that one can engage with them in the same way as one might with a voluntary client. If the client will not own the problem and/or feels that it is not his responsibility to change, the counsellor needs to find some benefit which attracts the client.

EXAMPLE

Counsellor: So what's brought you here today?
Client: My boss has been complaining about me. He says that if I don't change after coming here, then I'm going to lose my job.

Counsellor: How do you feel about that?

Client: I feel really angry. Why should I be the one who comes for counselling? I feel that I'm being blamed for the whole thing and I don't think that's fair.

Counsellor: You feel you've been unfairly blamed and that you don't see why you should be the one to change.

Client: That's right.

Counsellor: What would need to happen do you think before they stopped blaming you?

Client: I don't know.

[*Silence*]

Counsellor: You're not sure what they want from you.

Client: No.

Counsellor: What would they say if you asked them?

Client: That I don't let my personal problems interfere with my work, I suppose.

Counsellor: If you think that's how they see it, what would you notice that was different at work if they were interfering less?

Client: I wouldn't be off sick so often. I'd be enjoying my work again. At the moment I hate going in, I just don't want to be there.

Counsellor: What would be different for you if you were enjoying it just a bit better?

Client: I'd be out and about more and not stuck in the office all the time. That's the part of the job I like best, visiting the customers. I've known some of them for years. But they've taken me off that, until I sort my problems out.

Counsellor: What do you need to do to get that part of the job back?

Client: I need to prove that I'm more reliable.

Counsellor: How could you do that?

Client: By getting in on time, not being off sick. Coming back after lunch. Getting my paper work up to date.

Counsellor: Does any of that happen at the moment?

Client: It's been a bit of a bad patch recently. I'm usually very healthy, but it's just been one thing after the other.

Counsellor: You've been having a tough time. What do you think would be the first sign to your boss that you've started to be more reliable again?

Client: Being at my desk for 8.30 I suppose.

Counsellor: Is that something you want to do?

Client: Yes.

Counsellor: What would need to happen for that to happen?

Client: I used to always be the first in the place, I was dead keen. I'd need to tell myself that I had to do it if I wanted to get out of this mess.

Counsellor: How long will it be before you feel like that do you think?

Client: I feel like it now. It's just doing it.

In the first place, it is important for the counsellor to validate the client's perception of the situation, otherwise she will be seen by the client as a tool of the commissioning agency. This does not mean that one agrees with the client's version but it is an acknowledgement of the client's feelings and opinions. Second, it is essential to keep as closely as possible to the client's stated agenda (which may differ from that of the referral source). This helps to eliminate the 'yes but' exchanges which result when the client argues against any change in the status quo while the counsellor tries to propose ways forward. In SFT the client should work harder than the counsellor in constructing solutions and strategies towards achieving them. The 'one down' position of the counsellor ensures that she does not get ahead of the client in making suggestions on what the client might do. Third, the counsellor may need to seek the collaboration of the referring agency in negotiating goals for the client and supporting him in working towards them.

'Absent clients'   Many clients feel that their prospects of change are blighted by a key person in the system who refuses to acknowledge the problem or co-operate in solving it. This could be a partner who buries his or her head in the sand by denying or trivialising the problem; a colleague who has power over the client in the workplace; or a non-cooperative teenager. These partners in the client's life system are not customers for change; they refuse to accept the client's definition of the problem or to take responsibility for the consequences of their actions for other people. Despite the frustrations and hopelessness such a situation generates, the solution-focused questions in Figure 8.1 can be helpful.

Hudson and O'Hanlon (1991) suggest that on occasions it is possible to bring the absent party into the counselling if they can be reassured they will not be the focus of blame and they can be convinced that the counsellor really wants to hear their side of the story.

4   Is there a danger that SFT only addresses symptoms and does not deal with the underlying issues which may re-emerge later?

Durrant (1997), focusing upon the power of language in problem construction, states that there are only underlying issues if you talk about them in that way. The solution-focused conversation does allow for clients to offer explanations, make connections,

- Who wants change the most? What would the benefits of change be for everyone concerned?
- Who has the ability to deliver change?
- Where does the power lie and could its distribution be changed?
- Is there a different way of reading the situation which might help?
- What would constitute a reasonable improvement, even if the basic situation remained unaltered?
- What could the client change which she does have control over?
- What difference would it make if the client was able to make those changes?
- How can the client stop the situation getting worse?
- What might the short- and long-term options be?
- What would it mean for the client if she chose to accept some aspects of the situation?
- What could the client do that was different from what she usually does?
- Is the client trying too hard to change the situation?
- Would she be better off trying to do nothing for a while?
- Could the client stop the 'failed solutions' she has used?
- Who/what helps her to cope with this situation?
- How could she do more of what helps her to cope?
- Is she underestimating her power and overestimating the power of the other?
- How would she know this was happening?
- Have there been any times when she managed the situation even a little better?
- Is there any time when the other person acts in the way she wants, even for a few moments? If so, how did he do that?
- What difference did that make for the client?
- On a scale of zero to ten, where would she rate this problem today?
- What would need to happen for her to move up one point on the scale?
- How long does she think it will take before she sees some progress up the scale?
- Imagine the other person does not change at all, but a miracle happens for the client, what would be the signs for her that a miracle had happened?
- What does the client like about the way she is handling this very difficult situation?
- What will be the first signs for the client that the situation is showing some improvement?
- Could she study the situation more and report back to the counsellor when he does something that she would like to see continue?
- Is this as bad as it gets or is it likely to get worse?
- If so, how long would she want/be able to put up with it?
- When would she know she had had enough?
- What would need to happen for her to move up one point on the scale?

Figure 8.1   *Solution-focused questions when the 'client is absent'*

and identify past influences and events, but the solution-focused counsellor does not believe that current difficulties are resolved by identifying 'underlying issues'. The distinction between symptoms and underlying issues is in many respects unhelpful. Real and lasting personal change can begin anywhere – there is no one route to change. Achieving resolution of a current problem can give a very different perspective on the past; re-authoring (White 1995) the past can enable the future to become a different story; and constructing the future can influence the present (the miracle question). It should not be an automatic assumption that clients need to undertake the 'insight' route to change.

No form of counselling, not even the most analytical, claims to offer a definitive resolution of psychological problems. Successful counselling does not bring a guarantee of life-long happiness. Counsellors whose training taught them that the starting point with every client has to be the past and that the counsellor needs to assess the client's history carefully before entering into a contract, are likely to feel uneasy with a model which does not see the past as the necessary starting point. Such counsellors would claim that in their experience clients find it helpful to make links with, for example, patterns in families of origin which throw light on their current difficulties. With couples, time spent on family history can identify scripts which help to explain current tensions. The solution-focused therapist will acknowledge that what happened in the past was a problem then and may be influencing the current problem, but she will particularly highlight and reinforce what the clients have done to change their family scripts.

EXAMPLE

Counsellor: From what you've both told me, it sounds as if there was not much love or affection demonstrated in Jak's family when he was small, but more in yours Jean.

Jak: We're agreed on that. It's left me having difficulties showing affection to anyone. I'd like to be more demonstrative with the kids and with Jean, but it isn't easy, my dad never showed any affection to me.

Jean: You're not like your dad though Jak. He was more interested in things outside the home. He was just like a lot of dads at that time.

Counsellor: How do you feel you're different from your dad Jak?

Jak: I'm a lot more involved with the kids. If I have to go away on work I always speak to them on the phone every day. When I am at home we do a lot more things as a family. I know the things they're into . . . I've seen how Jean is always hugging and cuddling the kids. I'd like to do that more often, but I find I hold back. Having said that, I'm better than I used to be, now I sometimes cuddle them when we're sitting watching television. I couldn't do that a couple of years ago.

Counsellor: So it's not come as naturally to you as it did for Jean. Have you noticed Jean how much he has been trying?

Jean:: He's getting there. He's even getting round to kissing me when he comes and goes, that's progress!

Counsellor: Do you think Jak that being more affectionate towards Jean and showing more affection to the kids go together or do you see them as separate?

Jak: I never saw my mum and dad kiss, never. It was a shock when I went to Jean's house and saw her parents with their arms round each other. I think it's nice for children to see their parents love each other. I want my family life to be much warmer than mine was.

Counsellor: What's it like now when you cuddle the kids sometimes and give Jean a kiss when you come in or go out?

Jak: I like it, it's more like a real family.

Counsellor: Do you think you will keep this up and even get better at it over the next few months?

Jak: I'd like to be more spontaneous about it, at the moment it feels forced and awkward.

Counsellor: So to begin with, you have to think about it first then do it, but you'd like to get to the stage when you do it without thinking or planning it. It just happens.

Jak: Yes.

5   Is SFT naïve in that it takes the stories clients present at face value?

SFT works with the presenting problem (the client's agenda) and trusts the client. It does not try to read between the lines. SFT is more an attitude towards clients than a set of techniques. Just as it does not believe that more means better, nor does it believe that 'deep' somehow means more real or more significant. What is important is for the counsellor to create safe therapeutic time and space which allows the client to express what she wants in the way that she wants. If the counsellor succeeds, the client will disclose what she feels to be important when she feels it to be so. Any good counsellor realises how painful and difficult it is for clients to reveal aspects of themselves about which they feel ashamed or guilty or confused. Solution-focused counsellors do not interpret this as denial, rationalisation or resistance, but as

- Are you finding this helpful?
- Is this what you wanted to talk about?
- Is there anything else you want to tell me about?
- Is there anything you feel it would be important for me to know?
- Do you think I know enough in order to help?

Figure 8.2   *Evaluating progress*

the client pacing the type of co-operation which she feels is appropriate at this moment in time. In the experience of solution-focused counsellors, issues not initially disclosed – for example, abuse or discrimination – often emerge as the client begins to address the presenting problems. A growing sense of self-empowerment, perhaps linked to the respect and affirmation shown by the counsellor, can make it easier for the client to talk about 'the shadow side'. It is not so much a question of the counsellor raising or not raising 'hidden' issues but of how they are talked about and understood when they do arise. For many non-solution-focused counsellors, working without the tools which probe the client's past would provoke anxiety and a fear of missing the 'real' issue. It is only through training and supervision that they could begin to feel more comfortable with an approach which trusts the clients to talk about what they need to talk about.

6   Does the model address the issue of counsellor power and responsibility?
Different models generate different ethical dilemmas. Strategic family therapy and the MRI model (close relatives of SFT) have both been criticised in the past as being manipulative and devious. Clients were, for example, given paradoxical tasks – such as the prescription of their symptoms or being warned against getting better too soon. In SFT there is less reliance on giving clients unusual or 'tricky' assignments, and more emphasis on clients devising their own tasks. Practitioners choose 'to give their power away' by demystifying the therapeutic process and explaining to clients, in either pre-sessional literature or in the sessions themselves, exactly what the counselling entails so that clients can give their informed consent.

It is important that counsellors possess clear self-awareness and have engaged in personal development or therapy as part of their training, otherwise they may, wittingly or unwittingly, use the techniques of SFT in a directive and potentially unethical manner. Technical expertise without self-awareness can mask the unexpressed needs of the worker. Solution-focused ideas and practices developed in a family therapy setting in which co-workers were often, if not always, present and actively involved in the process. The relationship between the individual practitioner and the client was not sacred, with clients offered other counsellors if their own was unavailable for some reason. With team consultations, 'live supervision', the possibility of counsellors developing abusive relationships with clients was arguably less likely than in one-to-one situations, particularly in long-term therapy. Having said that, I acknowledge that therapist abuse has often taken place in a group context, particularly when a 'charismatic' dominant figure was the leader. Many counsellors who now use the method work on their own with only an external supervisor (see Chapter 7).

7   Is SFT suitable for cross-cultural work?

One way of understanding the 'one down' position of the counsellor is to see her as a 'guest' in the culture of the client. This attitude confers a respectful validation on the clients' perceptions and values, including their social context and stage of racial identity development. The emphasis on client strengths and competence helps the counsellor to affirm the client's cultural resources as part of the solution. The use of descriptive speech and a close adherence to the client's unique goals also help the solution-focused counsellor to respect diversity and avoid the imposition of the counsellor's values.

Data from the BFTC in Milwaukee (De Jong and Hopwood 1996) suggest that different racial groups show little difference in outcome and that client–counsellor racial mix is not related to the outcomes of SFT. The smallness of the subject group means that these findings must be treated with caution.

8   Does the emphasis on goals and solutions mean that the model particularly appeals to male counsellors and clients?

Some of the leading SFT practitioners are women, among them Weiner-Davis, Lipchik, Berg and Dolan. They have used the model with families, survivors of child abuse and victims of male violence. In the UK, Jane Lethem believes that the model 'has the capacity to validate the experiences of women, acknowledge the contribution of social injustice to many of their difficulties and offer them opportunities to utilize strengths they may have overlooked in resolving problems and dilemmas' (1994: 33).

De Jong and Hopwood (1996), in a small study which they warn needs to be read with caution, assert that women and men have equally positive outcomes, whether the counsellors using the model were men or women. Bailey-Martiniere (1993) argues that the model validates and communicates respect to women by:

1   listening without pathologising or interpreting her problem as a symptom of an underlying issue located in the past
2   viewing her as an expert with strengths and resources
3   using the miracle question to establish goals, rather than the ideas and biases of the counsellor about what a woman should or should not do
4   reframing problems as ordinary life experiences, liberating her from guilt and stereotypes such as victim and non-coper
5   equipping her with tools for change
6   avoiding endless emotional unburdening or analysis which can reinforce helplessness and depression
7   discouraging passivity, fatalism and self-defeating talk
8   helping women to articulate their own hopes and empowering them to act to create their own solutions.

These powerful qualities make the model eminently suitable for women clients and counsellors. Lethem (1994: 31) claims that the model respects both 'the tears and the desire for action'.

9

SFT and Eclecticism

In Chapter 2 I briefly referred to the different stages through which followers of new theories or systems of belief pass as they seek to propagate their ideas. According to Schwartz (1955), a defensiveness, coupled with an evangelical spirit, characterises the earlier stages. Tensions between different wings develop as the modernisers begin to modify the orthodox tradition in order to assimilate other progressive schools of thought. There are similar tensions within solution-focused therapy (SFT) between practitioners who advocate using only solution-focused methods and others who are more open to integrating with other therapies. My aim in this chapter is to explore how SFT could incorporate ideas and practices from other models which have different assumptions and aims.

It is generally recognised that while at the level of theory there are incompatible differences between different schools of therapy, at the practice level therapists are increasingly drawing upon a range of techniques without subscribing to the philosophy behind them. This technical eclecticism (Lazarus 1981) is atheoretical and pragmatic, which is consistent with SFT's emphasis on shedding unnecessary ideology and focusing on what works for the client. SFT advocates the principle of doing something different when therapy is stuck and this includes borrowing techniques from other models which are congruent with SFT values and beliefs.

The movement towards greater consensus and convergence between different therapeutic approaches is based upon the following evidence:

1   The theoretical orientation of the therapist is unimportant to clients, at least in comparison to the personality of the therapist, her experience, or the quality of the therapeutic relationship (Brown and Lent 1992).

2   Counsellors do not conform to the 'purist' theoretical models to which they subscribe (Schapp, Bennun, Schindler and Hoogduin 1993).
3   In general terms, there is equality of outcome between different approaches (research summarised in Garfield and Bergin 1994). No one model can claim superiority. Duncan (1992) criticises models which claim universal application and effectiveness. He suggests that the experience of counsellors is that nothing always works and that no one model is sufficient to address the complexity of the human condition or the uniqueness of individuals.
4   Lambert (1986) identified that as much as 30 per cent of outcome variance is related to common factors. He found that techniques were no more powerful than the placebo effect, both of which account for approximately 15 per cent of the positive outcome variance.
5   The emergence of brief therapy as the norm for practice has helped to identify a set of characteristics which most time-limited models have and which are more significant than any differences between them. These characteristics include:

- accepting people as competent
- forming the therapeutic alliance as quickly as possible
- giving the client credit for progress and success
- focusing on clear, specific, attainable goals
- projecting of the therapist as competent, hopeful and confident
- having a clear focus to the work
- accepting the client's view of the problem
- avoiding a power struggle with the client.

Person-centred therapy

At first sight there may appear to be little common ground between SFT and person-centred therapy. Some person-centred practitioners regard 'techniques' such as those used in SFT as fundamentally incompatible with a person-centred approach. Merry (1990) argues that therapist-initiated interventions constitute a breach of the 'here and now' quality of the counsellor–client encounter. This interference with the client's natural processes – for example, staying with painful experiences – he sees as arising from the insecurity and anxiety of the counsellor under pressure to produce results. As a consequence, 'the therapist's expertise, technique and power takes precedence over the client's personal power' (1990: 18).

Wilkins (1993) takes a more liberal line, distinguishing between person-centred *therapy*, which he sees as a therapeutic model with its own particular methodology, and a person-centred *approach*, which uses interventions congruent with person-centred core values, such as respect for the autonomy of the client. SFT meets this criterion because it enters into the client's frame of reference, disowns the role of expert, affirms and respects the client's experiences, builds on the client's essential healthiness, keeps close to the client's goals, and trusts the client to know how to overcome his problems and when to terminate. Payne (1993) sees the 'technique' of externalisation (see Chapter 5), which narrative and solution-focused therapy use, as being compatible with Rogerian values. In particular, he lists the common ground as being:

- a belief that clients always have the potential for self-derived growth and change
- a rejection of 'unconscious' explanations and processes as unknowable and of limited usefulness
- a belief that the central aim is to promote the empowerment of the client
- a range of positive, human, optimistic perspectives
- a conviction that clients have the ability to reorganise 'interiorised' experience as a route to overcoming problems.

SFT provides certain structures, such as the miracle question, scaling and exception seeking, which enable clients to explore their own feelings, thoughts and ideas about their lives. Every form of therapy, including person-centred, sets boundaries for the therapeutic encounter and seeks to influence the client. It is not possible to avoid influencing the client. It would be a strange use of resources if the client was not influenced by what happened in therapy. Influencing, while respecting client autonomy, is however different from directing the client according to what the counsellor considers to be right. For the above reasons I think it can be argued that SFT has a legitimate claim to consider itself to be person-centred.

The TFA model

Hutchins's (1989) TFA model is a useful integrating tool which the solution-focused counsellor can use to inform her solution-focused practice. Hutchins argues that counsellors need to be aware of both their clients' and their own dominant ways of experiencing the world. These modes he identifies as thinking, feeling and acting (TFA). Counsellors become aware of their clients' orientation by paying careful attention to how they talk about their problems. Although people are a mixture of all three elements, they are likely to have a bias towards one or another. He suggests that in order to form the therapeutic alliance counsellors should match the client's language, so that if the person speaks in feeling-oriented terms, the counsellor responds, at least initially, in kind. Matching modes of communication requires the counsellor to adapt to meet the client where she is, a principle congruent with the SFT custom of 'joining with' and learning from the client. If the counsellor knew that he personally had a strong action orientation and that the client had a strong feeling orientation, this would serve as a warning to the counsellor to avoid rushing towards solutions and rather to take time to validate and explore the client's feelings. If, however, the counsellor is predominantly a 'thinker' and the client a 'doer', he may waste time seeking a rationale for acting and hold the client back. Probably all good counsellors match their clients' language intuitively, but this framework helps them to do it in a more systematic and planned way. It helps the counsellor to make a productive start and to diffuse potential tensions and conflicts. The most effective counsellors will be those who adapt to a wide range of clients. Hutchins (1989) also advocates that counsellors should, at least initially, build upon the client's TFA strengths, an idea which clearly resonates with SFT. It is also important to be responsive to the dominant modes of the client in order to construct solutions which 'fit' the client. The increased self-awareness of the counsellor about her TFA profile can enable her to adapt the model to her personality rather than her personality to the model, although this point would not be accepted by some solution-focused practitioners. In my view, if the person is uneasy with aspects of the model her discomfort and incongruence will probably show and have negative effects on the therapeutic relationship.

Cycle of change model

SFT uses the categories of visitor, complainant and customer to describe the 'constructed positions' of clients in relation to change. The cycle of change model (Prochaska, Di Clemente and Norcross 1992), although it differs greatly from SFT in terms of theoretical assumptions, can be a useful tool for developing the solution-focused counsellor's thinking about the client's current readiness for change. The five-stage model describes a process, a cycle which people may go through as they attempt to change their behaviour. Progress is not linear. Individuals may revisit previous stages or remain stuck in one stage for a long time. The model takes into account that people usually have some form of problem relapse. The five stages are:

1   *Pre-contemplation*   At this stage a person may be a reluctant or involuntary client with little or no authentic motivation. The person may feel overwhelmed by the problem and unable to take the first step in what looks like a long and painful journey.
2   *Contemplation*   A contemplator wants to want to change his behaviour but may not feel ready to change and will procrastinate. He may have tried to change in the past but was unable to sustain the changes. He may need to see those 'failures' as temporary exceptions to the problem.
3   *Preparation*   The client has begun to plan seriously how he is going to overcome his problem. He has made preliminary decisions and engaged others to support him in the change process.
4   *Action*   The person has taken steps to make the changes he wants and has begun to implement his plan.
5   *Maintenance*   In this stage the client has some success in maintaining the problem-free behaviour, but may also have relapses and return to earlier phases of the cycle. Some people break out of the cycle altogether and no longer consider themselves to have the problem; others will feel they are on maintenance guard for a long time or even for the rest of their lives.

The cycle of change and SFT
A working knowledge of the model can help the solution-focused counsellor be aware of how to engage with the client:

- *Pre-contemplation*   Some of the strategies described in Chapter 8 for use with reluctant clients or with 'visitors' (de Shazer 1988) are relevant at this stage. These include: accepting the client's current ambivalence; not trying to argue for change; helping the client to formulate a goal; imagining with the client circumstances in which he might want to change.

- *Contemplation*   This is similar to the 'complainant' (de Shazer 1988) position in which the client identifies a problem or goal, but feels ambivalent or helpless when it comes to tackling it. Here the counsellor may remove the focus from the problem and emphasise instead competence, exceptions and the future as revealed through the miracle question. The client may not be ready for 'doing' tasks but may be willing to engage in 'noticing' tasks.

- *Preparation*   At this point the client is willing to think about possible solutions and to discuss 'what would need to happen for that to happen'. He may be willing to engage in 'experiments'. Setting clear, realistic and attainable goals and identifying both personal and environmental resources would be important.

- *Action*   The client is a 'customer for change' (de Shazer 1988). The counsellor reinforces constructive change and encourages the client to keep doing what is helpful.

- *Maintenance*   The solution-focused counsellor will have discussed maintenance strategies with the client and warned of possible relapses. They will have agreed a contingency plan. She may use scaling to highlight what the client did in order to stop the situation deteriorating further (if you were at one, how did you manage to stop it becoming zero?). She will continue to look for exceptions, and to help the client to learn from setbacks. The counsellor will help the client to construe what has happened in ways which do not trap him in the problem or disempower him in the face of failure. The counsellor may wish to explore with the client when and how he could discard his 'problem' identity, for example, as an alcoholic, anorexic or survivor of abuse.

As well as using ideas from other sources which can expand the solution-focused counsellor's thinking, there is a rich array of techniques in all fields of therapy which can be given a solution-focused twist. The following is a sample.

Integrating experiential techniques from other models

Experiential exercises are therapist-facilitated activities which provide the client with an immediate awareness-raising experience. There are a wide range of activities, including role playing, psychodrama, photo-therapy, fantasy and drawing. It is advisable to work with these techniques in a training situation before using them with clients.

Many types of therapy over-rely on the left side of the brain, which guides rationality, analysis and verbal fluency, but as Washburn (1994) points out, this mirroring of academia disenfranchises many people who operate in a predominantly right-sided (holistic, spatially oriented, non-verbal, artistic, intuitive) way and who may have a history of failure resulting from poor performance in left-sided tasks. He argues that brief solution-oriented therapy, 'with its focus on successes, tasks, concrete goals and assessment, is less likely to alienate the person with right brain dominance' (1994: 52). He sees SFT as having advantages for such people because it appeals to right brain functioning by emphasising concreteness rather than abstraction, action instead of insight. This may make it more user-friendly for people with learning or speech difficulties, or for children. For the practitioner the benefit of including non-verbal, experiential activities is that they facilitate access to people's emotional lives and act as a counterbalance to the inherent intellectualism of verbal therapies. Experiential activities can also ensure that the present is fully experienced as therapeutic and is not merely an exchange of information about past events or future goals. Another advantage of integrating experiential activities with SFT is that they can access feelings, ideas and memories which may not be reached by its normal form of questioning, limited as it is to the client's conscious awareness (Bischof 1993).

Drama

Bischof (1993) encourages clients to demonstrate situations where they experienced an exception to their problem, then to discuss what seemed to make the difference. He works in a similar way with the miracle question. He invites clients to imagine waking up after the miracle has happened and to act out some of the ensuing scenes, with the therapist taking the parts of family members, friends or colleagues. If anyone has accompanied the client to therapy, the client could sculpt the scene, positioning them according to how she envisages them after the miracle. An alternative method, when the client is reluctant to act out the scene, is to place coins or other objects on a table and for the client to move them to where they would be before and after the miracle and to explore his feelings and thoughts during the exercise.

Clients may also get in touch with their feelings and thoughts about where they are with their problem on the scale of zero to ten, by putting cards on the floor like stepping-stones or a horizontal ladder. The client stands along the continuum in relation to where he thinks he is today, moves to where he would like to get to, then explores what he would need to do to move up one point on the scale. The therapist can ask the client how he feels and what he is thinking as he stands at these various points.

Exercises from other experiential therapies can be adapted to fit the solution-focused orientation, for example, the empty chair sometimes used in Gestalt can be given a solution-oriented twist. The therapist suggests that the client constructs an imaginary dialogue with the absent person, concentrating upon competence, strengths, compliments, exceptions, goals and strategies. The scope is endless for therapists who are willing to improvise and spontaneously create learning situations.

Drawing

Experiential activities such as drawing or sculpting bypass inhibitions and generate ideas and feelings about solutions which were initially outside the client's awareness and verbal expression. Clients may be invited to draw scales, miracle scenarios or scenes which were exceptions to the problem. Sharing these with the therapist can elicit much helpful information. Children, in particular, may enjoy drawing pictures of ladders, stepping-stones or anything else which conveys movement to them. I have also experimented with encouraging clients to draw strip cartoons of miracles, exceptions, strengths and goals, and have been amazed at how inventive people can be.

Kuehl (1995) advocates using solution-oriented genograms with couples to represent visually clients' inter-generational relationships and thereby highlight family strengths, coping strategies, successes, exceptions and role models. Sharing genograms can enhance the couple's understanding of their experiences in their family of origin. Another helpful exercise is a solution-oriented discussion centred upon family photographs.

Letter writing

Many approaches advocate writing letters to clients and inviting clients to write letters or keep diaries. Some solution-focused therapists write to their clients following each session to summarise the content of the message and to reinforce the client's constructive actions. Sometimes clients request this, as they cannot remember clearly the feedback given at the end of the session.

As part of their 'homework' the therapist may ask clients to keep a record of occasions when they would have expected the problem to happen but it did not, or times when constructive things happened which they would like to see continue (first formula session task). They may include observations of other people's behaviour or detailed accounts of particular solution incidents. They may use a diary to keep note of their predictions or to record their day-to-day use of scaling. Anything which they do, say, think or feel which they consider to be helpful is recorded for feedback to the therapist. It becomes a record of solutions. This is clearly different from a diary which records the pattern of the problem. Nunnally and Lipchik (1989) describe using letters to clients as reminders of the task they are to do; as a supplement when something important was missed in the message at the end of the session; and as invitations for clarification of goals following a confusing session. Writing itself can be a therapeutic release which in turn alters the problem situations. Writing can be a form of 'doing something different'. I find it helpful for both client and counsellor to write about their experience at the end of a course of therapy. The following is a brief account written by a client at the end of therapy. He had been suffering from anxiety and panic attacks which affected his work performance, driving and home life.

I decided to seek help because I had not been able to resolve the situation myself after three years' struggling. I resisted getting help because I felt I could handle it alone – and if I wasn't able to handle it then I was worried I would be getting ill. Following a visit to my GP I began to take Paroxetene.

While the medication has not been the whole answer it has allowed me the space to put activities in place of anxieties.

The first thing which helped was realising that what I called 'symptoms' should more accurately be called 'signals'. These signals were signs sent to my body by my mind to tell me that my mind was having some difficulty in handling something. But mostly it was having difficulty handling the signals! So I needed to develop means to disregard the signals.

I developed a number of techniques for handling the immediate situation:

- ignore the feeling
- think of something else
- blank-out my mind
- picture something in my mind
- imagine a protective 'ring' around me or the car
- breathe slowly and feel my whole lungs fill, then slowly exhale
- stabilise my breathing to a steady rhythm.

While none of these things completely turned off the signals, they did reduce them to a point where I could get on with things and not spend time focusing on the signals. I have noticed that it seems to be worse when I have the time to sit and focus on it, then it is more difficult to get rid of it.

There seemed to be a point where the handling techniques 'kicked in'. The signals began to get shorter and shorter, less insistent, and the obsession which they normally produced which required me to concentrate on them began to subside until they were only there occasionally.

My real problem had been with driving. I began to drive again in all types of situations. I am now at the point where I can drive unaccompanied on the motorway.

I was glad we did not spend loads of time looking back into my past and asking what would have probably been fairly unfruitful questions about a past which could have been the cause of none or all of my problems and a few more.

The client described himself as 97 per cent recovered. His record of solutions, which he generated largely by himself, was a flexible repertoire he employed against panic attacks. He developed a 'firing order' in which he used them as well as realising that nothing worked for long and that it was important for him to vary his strategies.

In his summary he refers to, what was for him, a turning-point when he accepted the therapist's reframing of *symptoms* into *signals* which required an active response from him. The reframing included an externalisation of his anxiety as something which attacked him (sometimes when he was in a kind of trance), the signals being the first signs of the attack, rather than symptoms which implied an illness or condition over which he had little control. The client's attitude to medication enabled him to make the best possible use of the time to replace his old anxieties with 'activities' (his words), by which he meant strategies which he could continue to use once he had finished the medication.

Fantasy

A fantasy which I have used in a solution-focused way, the origins of which I do not know, is the Land of the Giants fantasy. In this the therapist invites the client to imagine that she has arrived in a land where everybody but the client is a giant. As she watches the giants play, work and do the kind of things that giants do, she needs to work out how she is going to meet her basic survival need. Some clients respond that they would lead a clandestine life, coming out only at night to scavenge. Others would take time to observe how the giants behave and then approach one who looks friendly. Others suggest visiting places where giants who share the same interests as them might be found – for example, bookshops, gardening centres, pubs and churches – in the hope of finding a soul brother or sister there. Very often the person doing the exercise assumes that all the giants are men, which in itself can raise interesting points for discussion! Some clients feel confident that the giants will like them and that they only need to ask for help for it to be forthcoming. Others suggest pleading for mercy or compassion, while others would try to impress the giants by presenting themselves as wise aliens with knowledge to share, or as fascinating creatures who could be entertaining court jesters. The fantasy discloses strategies which clients currently use in their lives, as well as strategies which were part of their life scripts but which are no longer appropriate. It also reveals many of the client's attitudes to life. The solution-focused perspective seeks to find strategies which have worked in the past and are transferable, and to identify old scripts which need discarding, as well as those strengths and values which could contribute towards the solution.

Problem-solving techniques

Lazarus's (1981) technique of inviting clients to state their problem in one word, then to put it into the context of one sentence can be very useful. Even when clients are not able to find the 'right' word, the technique helps to give an immediate focus to the work and often reveals key feelings and concerns. If possible the solution-focused therapist will convert the initial problem statement into a goal statement.

EXAMPLE

> *Client*: The one word would be 'failure' and the sentence would be 'I am a complete failure in making relationships with members of the opposite sex'.
> *Therapist*: So up till now you feel you have not had much success in these relationships and you would like counselling to help you improve them. What will be the first signs for you that you are beginning to make better relationships?

Force-field analysis

Egan (1990) incorporated this technique into his three-stage model. Counsellor and client identify the positive and negative forces which are either facilitating or hindering the client from achieving her goals. Having identified and prioritised both sets of forces they explore strategies to maximise the positives and minimise the negatives (Figure 9.1).

The forces restraining the client from achieving her goal might include the way in which she thinks about the problem, her attachment to failed solutions and her fears that taking risks might make the situation worse. Her social network may be a powerful reinforcer of these negative constraints. In order to develop facilitative strategies, the counsellor will need to help the client to find alternative ways of thinking about the problem and to encourage and support her 'to do something different'. SFT reinforces facilitating processes by building upon strengths and exceptions. It constantly seeks out resources, both personal and environmental, and stresses client competence. Unless this work

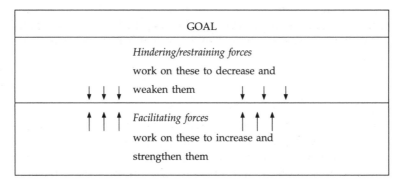

Figure 9.1   *Force-field analysis*

is accomplished with a strong sense of realism it may develop into myopic optimism, resulting in the client underestimating the difficulties involved in making changes and consequently giving up when change proves more difficult than anticipated. In my view incorporating a negative focus into strategy-setting increases the realism with which the client tackles the problem. A solution-focused use of force-field analysis might employ the questions shown in Figure 9.2.

There are of course some restraining forces over which the client has no control, for example, economic policy and its effect on employment practices. However, even then, the client may find opportunities to join with others to work towards political and social change.

Brainstorming
SFT makes constant use of people's imaginations – the miracle question, predictions, rehearsals and visualisations, for example. One of its strong points is its ability to generate solutions with clients and brainstorming can be used to do this. For brainstorming to be effective there are usually ground rules, such as:

- Write down every suggestion.
- Do not criticise any suggestion.
- Encourage quantity – evaluate quality later.
- Combine suggestions to make new ones.
- When finished, leave list aside; return to it later to add to it or to refine it.

- When, where and how will obstacles arise to block you?
- What will be the first signs for you that you've met an obstacle?
- What do you think will be the hardest thing for you as you make these changes?
- What have you learned from your past experience of difficulties which will help you?
- How do you think other people will respond once you start to change?
- How will you remember what to do when you feel discouraged?
- What will you say to yourself at those times?
- Who would be a resource for you at that time?
- What would you do if you discovered that you take two steps forward then one step back?
- Do you think that your situation is as bad as it will get or do you think it could get worse?
- Even if you cannot solve the situation, what would you need to do to stop it getting worse?
- On a scale of zero to ten, ten being you are absolutely confident you can overcome these obstacles, where are you today and is that good enough?

Figure 9.2   *Solution-focused questions about negative forces*

Uncensored, imaginative, freely associated brainstorming can lead in directions which logical, linear thinking does not access. The counsellor can help the client to refine the options by referring back to exceptions and examples of client competence. Both should contribute to the brainstorming but the counsellor's principal role is to stimulate and support the client.

If SFT can enrich itself by borrowing from other traditions, what can SFT ideas and practices add to the work of practitioners who wish to incorporate them into their way of working?

1   SFT may prompt counsellors to reconsider the balance of time which they spend in discussing the past, the present and the future. Techniques such as scaling and the miracle question can help counsellors and clients to move on when they have become stuck in problem exploration.

2   Having a curiosity about the client's coping strategies can act as a corrective to the bias which treats clients as sick or inadequate. It can act also as an antidote to problem-focused thinking which obscures the client's ingenuity and inventiveness.

3   SFT invites counsellors to consider that it is not always necessary to start therapy by exploring the past or to look for causes and explanations for the client's problem.

4   It reminds counsellors of the importance of concrete, descriptive speech, particularly with clients tempted to 'live in their heads'. It also encourages a 'matching' between client and counsellor speech.

5   It fosters awareness of the social reality in which the therapeutic conversation takes place and in particular of how therapy is co-constructed. It highlights how the use of language can determine the length of therapy or make problems appear solvable or unsolvable.

6   It encourages counsellors to trust the client.

7   It respects the power of clients in relation to their goals and in their choice about when to end the counselling.

8   Its flexibility over the length and frequency of sessions raises possibilities for counsellors who tend to see most clients weekly for a 'fifty-minute hour'.

9   Its minimalism reminds counsellors about boundaries and the dangers of dependency.

10 Its emphasis on the value of 'joining with' the client and not engaging in confrontational behaviour promotes creative ways of entering into the client's frame of reference. Many of the above ideas and practices could be integrated into other forms of therapy without undermining the core beliefs of the counsellor.

10

Applications of SFT

It is possible to adapt solution-focused therapy (SFT) principles for use in a wide range of settings, such as education, health and social work (residential and field), as well as with small groups and organisations. In this chapter I will suggest some features of this work.

Groups

Any group can be run on solution-focused lines. The literature describes groups for parents (Selekman 1991), couples (Zimmerman et al. 1997), patients (Vaughn, Hastings and Kassner 1996; Chevalier 1995), supervisees (Thomas 1994) and staff (Goldberg and Szyndler 1994). Some of the advantages for facilitators and members of SFT groups are:

1   The emphasis on strengths, successes and compliments creates a non-blaming, positive climate in the group.
2   The affirmation of members' achievements in the presence of peers raises self-esteem.
3   The outward-looking, future orientation of the group generates more energy and ideas than a problem-focused one.
4   A group trained to look for exceptions and strengths can become a powerful source of social and moral support for the individual.
5   The specificity of goals both for the members and the group as a whole provides a focus for monitoring progress and avoids time-wasting irrelevancies.
6   The focus on small changes creates a positive momentum in the group.

7   The egalitarian nature of SFT encourages everyone to take responsibility for the group, with the role of the leader being more to ask the questions than to provide the answers.

8   The active participation in other people's search for solutions can help the person to become more aware of their own. It may be possible to borrow someone else's solution.

9   People who find it difficult to talk about their problems in front of others are often more willing to talk about solutions. The non-confrontational nature of an SFT group encourages freer expression from the members.

10   The absence of analysis and interpretation reduces members' anxiety levels.

11   The descriptive and concrete questions of SFT help to engage people who would struggle with abstract discussions.

12   There is an emphasis on utilising all the resources in the group. The group support and dynamic can help the individual to carry out tasks and counterbalance possible negative and pessimistic messages from other quarters.

13   Experiential solution-focused exercises can be used to greater effect than in one-to-one work.

14   The rejection of labels and a wariness about diagnosis helps to remove the stigma of group membership. It is not a group for people with problems but one for people looking for solutions.

15   The group can develop its own rituals for celebrating successes.

Groups which are run on solution-focused principles will:

- create an expectation of change
- find as many different ways of describing and understanding problems as possible
- do something different if stuck
- look for difference and magnify it
- seek 'skeleton' solutions which fit many different problems
- focus on strengths, transferable skills and exceptions to the problem
- accept the client's definition of the problem
- be goal-oriented
- believe in the clients
- begin with small steps towards change.

- There is a shared 'vision'.
- Management trusts the workforce, treats people well and expects the best from them.
- It develops each employee's talents and expertise and builds on their strengths.
- It emphasises co-operation and collaboration between colleagues and departments.
- It consults at every level.
- It does what it can do best.
- It clearly defines aims and objectives.
- It strikes a balance between micro- and macro-planning.
- It examines and discards outdated traditions.
- It generates a creative atmosphere.
- It recognises and rewards employees' achievements.
- It emphasises personal responsibility and stake-holding.
- It spends more time in solution construction than in problem exploration.
- It develops staff's interpersonal communication skills.
- It runs purposeful and efficient meetings.
- It has fair and equal personnel policies.
- It provides welfare services for staff.

Figure 10.1   *Characteristics of the solution-focused organisation*

Organisations

I have taught solution-focused skills to managers, administrators, personnel officers, health and safety officers, and staff support teams, as well as to trade union shop stewards. Solution-focused skills and values can enhance the culture of the workplace and improve communication and problem-solving. The solution-focused organisation would be recognisable by those characteristics listed in Figure 10.1.

Organisations can profitably explore the miracle question and scaling in relation to their core activities. Many organisations are hampered by what they have inherited or accumulated over the years. The miracle question enables staff to think how they would do things differently if they were to make a new start the following day. Since it moves between fantasy and reality, the miracle question tends to bypass the negativity and lethargy which prevent people in some organisations imagining that things could ever be different or better. The following questions can be helpful:

- If we came in to work tomorrow and the business/agency/ organisation had been transformed overnight into the kind of organisation we would like to be, what would be the first signs we would notice?

- What would we be doing that was different?
- What would we have stopped doing?
- What would the miracle look like to senior management, middle management, project leaders, the cleaners, the personnel department, administration, the finance department?
- What difference would it make?
- How would our customers/users/clients notice the difference?
- How would it have come about?
- What would have been the first thing that would have changed?
- What would need to happen for some of those things to happen?
- Where would we start?
- What would be the gains for various people?
- Taking each aspect of the changes, on a scale of zero to ten where are we now in relation to making them happen?
- Is that good enough?
- Where do we want to get to?
- How could we move one point further up the scale?
- If one part of the organisation moved up the scale how would that affect other departments?

Employee Assistance Programmes

The brief solution-focused model ideally suits the mushrooming Employee Assistance Programmes (EAPs) provided by most large companies. These programmes typically offer a range of services to employees, from legal, financial and career advice, to critical incident debriefing and telephone and face-to-face counselling. Each EAP is different because of the differing needs of companies and the diversity of contracts. However, they share a common denominator of counselling being time-limited, with four to eight sessions being typical. Employers may fear (without good cause) that their employees would prolong counselling given the choice. With short-term contracts comes the responsibility for the counsellor, whether they be employed in-house or by an external provider, to make maximum use of the available time. This requires the mind set and skills repertoire described in Chapter 1 on brief therapy. These include:

- thorough assessment
- rapid formation of the therapeutic alliance
- keeping close to the client's agenda
- focusing on a central issue
- realistic goal setting
- utilisation of the client's resources
- generation of problem-solving strategies
- evaluation of success
- planned endings.

SFT research (McDonald 1994, Kiser 1988, De Jong and Hopwood 1996) suggests that the typical number of sessions, even in settings where there is no rationing of services, is between three and six, which makes it an attractive model for workplace counsellors.

Many EAP clients present in crisis with specific work or personal issues, such as redundancy, workplace bullying or harassment, stress, or personal relationship/health/life-event difficulties. In the main, they do not want long-term exploratory counselling; they need someone with whom they can think through their problem who is independent and non-judgemental and who will help them to decide what the next steps should be. They are, therefore, well disposed towards solution construction as they have felt stuck and unable to move forward on their own. The fact that company contracts stipulate the number of sessions to which the client is entitled can provide a natural boundary for the work and spur the client on to invest time and energy in tackling it. Where EAP counsellors cannot help clients within the limitations of the contract, they need to refer them to other sources which can offer long-term or specialised help. Although this sounds simple the reality of such referrals can be difficult for the client, who feels reluctant to restart with another counsellor, and for the counsellor, who may feel frustrated, anxious and guilty about not completing the work with the client. To some extent, such cases should be identified at the assessment stage, but even cases which initially appear suitable for brief work can turn out to require more time than envisaged.

- Belief in the resourcefulness of its pupils.
- Commitment to the values of respect, diversity and fairness.
- Positive management of change.
- Preoccupation with success and giving credit to people.
- Sense of collaboration and partnership in learning.
- Commitment to empower pupils by imparting the key skills of numeracy, literacy, and IT.
- Sense of the school as part of the local community involving parents, community groups, local businesses and others who can contribute to the life of the school.
- Climate of accountability and responsibility, and avoidance of blame and destructive criticism.
- Clear targets and goals for staff, pupils and the school as an organisation.
- Open appraisal and auditing systems.
- Whole school anti-bullying policy and use of peer counsellors.
- Good liaison with other professional groups, such as social workers and psychologists.
- Wide use of devolved powers.
- Use of gifted teachers to facilitate other teachers' search for solutions.

Figure 10.2 *Characteristics of a solution-focused school*

Education

Kral (1986), Durrant (1993b), Rhodes and Ajmal (1995) and others have written about using solution-focused ideas in consultations with teachers, in school management and in direct work with pupils. In my own experience, teachers, psychologists and educational social workers with large classes, limited resources or heavy caseloads, constant crises and little time, have warmly welcomed the simplicity and discipline of SFT. Much of what SFT advocates is already being done by good educationalists. Figure 10.2. describes the characteristics of a solution-focused school (and the government policies behind it).

Student counselling services in colleges and universities are increasingly recognising that a high proportion of their clients only attend for less than six sessions and that their counsellors need to be equipped for working in this way. As a tutor in a college of higher education, I find that solution-focused ideas are very helpful in tutorials and seminars with students. All my students are mature students returning to study after a long break or having no previous experience of academic work at tertiary level. Since the course is a professional counselling training, they are likely to experience feelings of being de-skilled in the early stages, as they unlearn old ways and integrate new ways. Aspects of the academic or clinical work can bring a temporary loss of confidence, power and status, with resulting confusion, anxiety, anger and fear.

A solution-focused perspective, while validating their anxieties and fears, builds respectfully upon the experiences, values, skills and learning styles which they bring to the course. It helps them to formulate realistic learning objectives. Its attention to micro-planning is useful when organising study patterns or writing essays. It is helpful for reducing perceived mountains into small hills, to be scaled one at a time. It reminds the tutor of the importance of giving constructive and encouraging feedback to students while at the same time 'joining with' the student to find ways forward for further improvement. When solution-focused ideas permeate an entire course, it becomes a learning community in which there is a sense of partnership characterised by energy, purpose and mutual respect.

Health

Health workers such as community psychiatric nurses, clinical psychologists, nurse therapists and counsellors in primary care, as well as others working in the voluntary sector, have shown considerable enthusiasm for using solution-focused ideas with patients with mental or physical illnesses (Webster 1990, Twyn 1992, Mason, Breen and Whipple 1994 and Vaughn, Cox Young, Webster and Thomas 1996).

SFT beliefs and methods challenge the construction of medical labels and emphasise the active change-agent role patients have in managing their illness. SFT defends the individual's unique and changing experience of illness and seeks to utilise the person's self-healing powers. Goldberg and Szyndler (1994) describe how staff in a paediatric ward use the method to generate an increased number of solutions to problems by building upon staff knowledge and skills and increasing the variety of staff interactions with patients, their families and between staff themselves. According to Vaughn et al. (1996: 102),

> Solution-focused therapy is consistent with the aims of nursing interventions, including building clients' trust, promoting their sense

of control and positive orientation, affirming and supporting their strengths, and setting health-oriented mutual goals.

A solution-focused approach to health adopts a 'holistic' stance which links body, mind and spirit with the social environment of the person. A holistic approach taps all the unused or underused resources of the client.

SFT can be used with patients suffering from physical or mental problems. Its attention to small steps makes it user-friendly for patients with chronic or even terminal illness. There are elements in any illness over which patients have no control and with which they need to come to terms, but there are many other aspects which require a more active response. The counsellor tries to discover what patients are or are not doing when the pain is less acute (exceptions), and what the patients are already doing which is helpful or at least preventing the illness getting worse (coping strategies). Patients may have psychological resources (thought stopping, diversionary thoughts, visualisations) of which they are unaware, but which they need to trigger to divert negative thoughts. How people understand and relate to their illness or pain and how they and others construct their 'sick role' are crucial determinants in how they cope. They can use scaling to identify realistic goals and to monitor the micro-steps towards their goals. Although the answer to the miracle question might be an unattainable cure, there will inevitably be things which the client would like to do, or want others to do or refrain from doing, which do not require a miracle. In terminal illness in particular, patients may have a clear idea how they would like the precious time remaining to be spent.

Social work

There are many difficult issues to be resolved in the interface between the statutory roles of the social worker and the need for families and children to participate in genuinely therapeutic work which require much lengthier treatment than this book allows. Solution-focused ideas are being used by social workers (George et al. 1990) who provide direct services to families, young people and children. They have been used in residential work (Durrant 1993a), and with survivors of abuse (Dolan 1991, McConkey 1992). The solution-focused approach has much to offer social workers:

- Solution-oriented questions can help to shift a potentially overwhelming preoccupation with problems into more productive areas.
- Its descriptive language and lack of analysis is useful in defining a focal issue and agreeing realistic goals.
- Its step-by-step approach helps to guide workers and clients through a maze of inter-connected multiple problems.
- It draws attention to the fact that the clients have survived previous crises and it attempts to discover how they coped and whether they could reactivate those strategies.
- It is a respectful approach which utilises the strengths, skills and values of the client.
- Its emphasis on collaboration and empowerment of the client reduces hostility and 'resistance'.
- It has practical tools for use with involuntary and 'absent' clients (see Chapter 8).

Dolan has developed a practical, sensitive and imaginative solution-focused approach to working with survivors of abuse. In her view, as well as listening and acknowledging the client's story,

> It is equally important that therapy not be limited to the tasks of recounting the details of the abuse and sorting out and acknowledging the resultant feelings. In order to respectfully and effectively address the client's treatment needs, therapy needs to include and strongly emphasize an active utilization of the client's present life resources and images of future goals and possibilities. (1991: 25)

She uses a solution-focused recovery scale which lists many ordinary day-to-day activities which the client has begun which are signs of healing and others which are realistic goals for her (1991: 32).

The Probation Service

The primary thrust of policy in the Probation Service is currently one of confronting offenders with their behaviour in order to elicit from them a greater sense of responsibility. To that end offenders are often mandatorily sent to specific treatment groups (such as anger management, alcohol and drug abuse, sex offenders) with pre-set programmes designed to tackle their offending behaviour and which do not often consider the personal agenda of their members. While it is clearly important that offenders take ownership of their behaviour, it is also important that too much attention is not given to negatives and past offences which can foster a defensive victim mentality which projects blame on to others. This in turn can lead to the offender refusing to take blame either for past or future behaviour. A focus on the past (the crime) is of little value unless it can also focus on what clients want for the future (provided it is legal) and how they could begin, step by step, to construct that future, given the limitations imposed as a consequence of their criminal past.

A solution-focused approach balances the 'correctional' function with one which validates the constructive and positive aspects of the person upon which a non-offending future might be built. It favours discussions with clients which explore exceptions to the offending behaviour, discovers what they are already doing which reduces or stops their offending and utilises their skills and strengths. It is more personalised and realistically hopeful. Solution-focused techniques for gaining the co-operation of involuntary clients (Chapter 8) can be useful. Probation officers who have a solution-focused perspective in their work report that they have been surprised at how much their clients have responded to a more respectful, client-centred approach. Such an approach would be one which identifies what the client needs to be doing or not doing instead of committing offences and which describes what the magistrate or probation officer needs to see to be convinced that change is taking place; one which gives clients positive feedback and encourages them in using their resources to build a better future for themselves.

The Probation Service works not only with offenders but with couples whose relationship has ended and who are unable to reach an agreement about contact and residence in relation to their children. Acting as Family Court Welfare Officers, probation staff prepare reports for the Court on these contentious issues. Couples are frequently engaged in recriminatory behaviour towards each other with the children being caught up in the conflict and sometimes used as pawns. When parties attend for interview the atmosphere is often acrimonious and confrontational. The task of the Family Court Welfare Officer is to write a report which focuses upon the welfare of the children. In an atmosphere of blame, anger, fear, confusion, anxiety and hurt, solution-focused questions can help the couple find ways forward in constructing an acceptable solution for the children.

Appendix
Trainers in SFT

Bill O'Connell
Focus on Solutions
97 Glyn Farm Rd
Quinton
Birmingham
B32 1NJ
0121 422 2525

Brief Therapy Practice
4d Shirland Mews
London
W9 3DY
0181 968 0070

Dave Hawkes
CMHT Four
The Willows
St George's Hospital
Suttons Lane
Hornchurch
Essex
RM12 6RS
01708 465034

Harry Norman
29 Wesley Place
Clifton
Bristol
BS8 4YD
0117 968 2417

Christina Saunders
35 Chilworth Mews
London
W2 3RG
0171 262 8718

Ron Wilgosh
4 Barrington Court
Hutton
Brentwood
Essex
CM13 IAX
01277 200544

References

Adams, J., Piercy, F. and Jurich, J. (1991) Effects of solution focused therapy's 'formula first session task' on compliance and outcome in family therapy. *Journal of Marital and Family Therapy*, 17 (3): 277–90.

Adler, A. (1925) *The Practice and Theory of Individual Psychology*. London: Routledge and Kegan Paul.

Alexander, F. and French, T.M. (1946) *Psychoanalytic Therapy*. New York: Ronald Press.

Allen, J. (1993) The constructionist paradigm: values and ethics. In J. Laird (ed.), *Revisioning Social Work Education: A Social Constructionist Approach*. New York: Haworth Press.

Anderson, H. and Swim, S. (1995) Supervision as collaborative conversation: connecting the voices of supervisor and supervisee. *Journal of Systemic Therapies*, 14 (2): 1–13.

Ardrey, R. (1970) *The Social Contract; A Personal Enquiry into the Evolutionary Sources of Order and Disorder*. New York: Athenaeum.

Bachelor, A. (1988) How clients perceive therapist empathy. *Psychotherapy*, 25: 227–40.

Bailey-Martiniere, L. (1993) Solution-oriented psychotherapy – the 'difference' for female clients, News of the Difference, II (2): 10–12.

Bandler, R. and Grinder, J. (1979) *Frogs into Princes*. Moab, UT: Real People Press.

Barkham, M. (1993) Counselling for a brief period. In W. Dryden (ed.), *Questions and Answers for Counselling in Action*. London: Sage.

Barret-Kruse, C. (1994) Brief counselling: a user's guide for traditionally trained counsellors. *International Journal for the Advancement of Counselling*, 17: 109–15.

Bateson, G. (1972) *Steps to an Ecology of Mind*. New York: Ballantine.

Berg, I.K. (1991) *Family Preservation – A Brief Therapy Workbook*. London: Brief Therapy Press.

Berg, I.K. (1994) *Family Based Services*. New York: Norton.

Berg, I.K. and de Shazer, S. (1993) Making numbers talk: language in therapy. In S. Friedman (ed.), *New Language of Change*. New York: Guilford Press.

Berg, I.K. and Miller, S.D. (1992) *Working with the Problem Drinker: A Solution Focused Approach*. New York: W.W. Norton.

Bernstein, B. (1972) Social class, language and socialization. In P.P. Giglioli (ed.), *Language and Social Context*. Harmondsworth: Penguin.

Beutler, L. and Crago, M. (1987) Strategies and techniques of prescriptive psychotherapeutic intervention. In R. Hales and A. Frances (eds), *Psychiatric*

Updates: The American Psychiatric Association Annual Review. Washington: American Psychiatric Press.

Bischof, G. (1993) Solution focused brief therapy and experiential family therapy activities: an integration. *Journal of Systemic Therapies*, 12 (3): 61–72.

Bloom, B.L. (1981) Focused single session therapy: initial development and evaluation. In S. Budman (ed.), *Forms of Brief Therapy*. New York: Guilford Press.

Bloom, B.L. (1992) *Planned Short Term Psychotherapy*. Boston: Allyn and Bacon.

Brech, J. and Agulnik, P. (1996) Do brief interventions reduce waiting times for counselling? *Counselling*, 7 (4): 322–6.

British Association for Counselling (1996) *Code of Ethics and Practice for Counsellors*. Rugby: BAC Publications.

Brown, S.D. and Lent, R.W. (1992) *Handbook of Counselling Psychology*. New York: Wiley.

Budman, S.H. and Gurman, A. (1988) *Theory and Practice of Brief Therapy*. New York: Guilford Press.

Budman, S.H. and Gurman, A. (1992) A time sensitive model of brief counselling: the I-D-E approach. In S.H. Budman, M. Hoyt and S. Friedman (eds), *The First Session in Brief Counselling*. New York: Guilford Press.

Butler, W. and Powers, K. (1996) Solution-focused grief therapy. In S. Miller, M. Hubble and B. Duncan (eds), *Handbook of Solution Focused Brief Therapy*. San Francisco: Jossey-Bass.

Cade, B. and O'Hanlon, W. (1993) *A Brief Guide to Brief Therapy*. New York: W.W. Norton.

Cantwell, P. and Holmes, S. (1995) Cumulative process: a collaborative approach to systemic supervision. *Journal of Systemic Therapies*, 14 (2): 35–46.

Chevalier, A.J. (1995) *On the Client's Path: A Manual for the Practice of Solution Focused Therapy*. Oakland: New Harbinger Publications Inc.

Cummings, N. and Sayama, M. (1995) *Focused Psychotherapy*. New York: Brunner/Mazel.

Davanloo, H. (ed.) (1980) *Short Term Dynamic Psychotherapy*. New York: Jason Aronson.

De Jong, P. and Hopwood, L. (1996) Outcome research on treatment conducted at the Brief Family Therapy Center, 1992–3. In S. Miller, M. Hubble and B. Duncan (eds), *Handbook of Solution Focused Brief Therapy*. San Francisco: Jossey-Bass.

de Shazer, S. (1984) The death of resistance. *Family Process*, 23: 11–17.

de Shazer, S. (1985) *Keys to Solutions in Brief Therapy*. New York: W.W. Norton.

de Shazer, S. (1988) *Clues: Investigating Solutions in Brief Therapy*. New York: W.W. Norton.

de Shazer, S. (1994) *Words were Originally Magic*. New York: W.W. Norton.

de Shazer, S. (1996) Presentation on solution focused therapy. Glasgow. Organised by the Brief Therapy Practice. July 1996.

de Shazer, S. and Berg, I.K. (1992) Doing therapy: a post-structural re-vision. *Journal of Marital and Family Therapy*, 18 (1): 71–81.

de Shazer, S. and Berg, I.K. (1997) 'What works?' Remarks on research aspects of solution focused therapy. *Journal of Family Therapy*, 19: 121–4.

de Shazer, S., Berg, I.K., Lipchik, E., Nunnally, E., Molnar, A., Gingerich, W. and

Weiner-Davis, M. (1986) Brief therapy: focused solution development. *Family Process*, 25: 207–21.

de Shazer, S. and Molnar, A. (1984) Four useful interventions in brief family therapy. *Journal of Marital and Family Therapy.* 10 (3): 297–304.

Dolan, Y. (1991) *Resolving Sexual Abuse: Solution Focused Therapy and Ericksonian Hypnosis for Adult Survivors.* New York: W.W. Norton.

Duncan, B. (1992) Strategic therapy, eclecticism and the therapeutic relationship. *Journal of Marital and Family Therapy*, 18 (1): 17–24.

Durrant, M. (1993a) *Residential Treatment: A Co-operative Competency-based Approach to Therapy and Program Design.* New York: W.W. Norton.

Durrant, M. (1993b) *Creative Strategies for School Problems.* Epping, NSW: Eastwood Family Therapy Centre.

Durrant, M. (1997) Presentation on brief solution focused therapy. London. Organised by the Brief Therapy Practice.

Eckert, P. (1993) Acceleration of change: catalysts in brief therapy. *Clinical Psychology Review*, 13: 241–53.

Egan, G. (1990) *The Skilled Helper.* 4th edn. Pacific Grove, CA: Brooks/Cole.

Eliot, T.S. (1963) *Collected Poems 1909–1962.* London: Faber and Faber.

Erickson, M.H. (1980) *Collected Papers. Vols 1–4* (E. Rossi, ed.). New York: Irvington.

Fanger, M. (1993) After the shift: time effective treatment in the possibility frame. In S. Friedman (ed.), *The New Language of Change.* New York: Guilford Press.

Ferenczi, S. and Rank, O. (1925) *The Development of Psychoanalysis.* New York: Dover.

Fisch, R. (1994) Basic elements in the brief therapies. In M. Hoyt (ed.), *Constructive Therapies.* New York: Guilford Press.

Fisch, R., Weakland, J.H. and Segal, L. (1982) *The Tactics of Change – Doing Therapy Briefly.* San Francisco: Jossey-Bass.

Frances, A., Clarkin, J. and Perry, S. (1984) *Differential Therapeutics in Psychiatry: The Art and Science of Treatment Selection.* New York: Brunner/Mazel.

Freedman, J. and Combs, G. (1993) Invitations to new stories: using questions to explore alternative possibilities. In S. Gilligan and R. Price (eds), *Therapeutic Conversations.* New York: W.W. Norton. pp 291–303.

Gale, J. and Newfield, N. (1992) A conversation analysis of a solution focused marital therapy session. *Journal of Marital and Family Therapy*, 18 (2): 153–65.

Garfield, S.L. and Bergin, A.E. (1994) *Handbook of Psychotherapy and Behavioral Change.* New York: Wiley.

George, E., Iveson, C. and Ratner, H. (1990) *Problem to Solution.* London: BT Press.

Goldberg, D. and Szyndler, J. (1994) Debating solutions: a model for teaching about psychosocial issues. *Journal of Family Therapy*, 16: 209–17.

Howard, K.I., Kopta, S., Krause, M. and Orlinsky, D. (1986) The dose effect relationship in psychotherapy, *American Psychologist*, 41: 159–64.

Hoyt, M. (1995) *Brief Therapy and Managed Care.* San Francisco: Jossey-Bass.

Hudson, P. and O'Hanlon, W. (1991) *Rewriting Love Stories.* New York: W.W. Norton.

Hutchins, D.E. (1989) Improving the counselling relationship. In W. Dryden (ed.), *Key Issues for Counselling in Action.* London: Sage.

Inskipp, F. (1996) New directions in supervision. In R. Bayne, I. Horton and J. Bimrose (eds), *New Directions in Counselling.* London: Routledge.

Inskipp, F. and Proctor, B. (1989) *Being Supervised: Audio tape 1, Principles of Counselling*. St Leonard's-on-Sea: Alexia Publications.

Janis, I. (1983) *Short-Term Counselling, Guidelines on Recent Research*. New Haven: Yale University Press.

Kelly, G.A. (1955) *The Psychology of Personal Constructs*. New York: W.W. Norton.

Kiser, D. (1988) A follow up study conducted at the Brief Family Therapy Center. Unpublished manuscript.

Kiser, D. and Nunnally, E. (1990) The relationship between treatment length and goal achievement in solution focused therapy. Unpublished manuscript.

Kiser, D., Piercy, F. and Lipchik, E. (1993) The integration of emotion in solution focused therapy. *Journal of Marital and Family Therapy*, (19) 3: 233–42.

Kleckner, T., Frank, L., Bland, C., Amendt, J. and Du Ree Bryant, R. (1992) The myth of the unfeeling strategic therapist. *Journal of Marital and Family Therapy*, 18 (1): 41–51.

Kogan, L.S. (1957) The short term case in a family agency. *Social Casework*, 38: 366–74.

Koss, M.P. and Butcher, J.N. (1986) Research on brief psychotherapy. In S.L. Garfield and A.E. Begin (eds), *Handbook of Psychotherapy and Behavior Change*. 3rd edn. New York: Wiley.

Kral, R. (1986) Indirect therapy in schools. In S. de Shazer and R. Kral (eds), *Indirect Approaches in Therapy*. Rockville, MA: Aspen.

Kral, R. and Kowalski, K. (1989) After the miracle: the second stage in solution focused brief therapy. *Journal of Strategic and Systemic Therapies*, 8 (2): 73–6.

Kuehl, B. (1995) The solution-oriented genogram: a collaborative approach. *Journal of Marital and Family Therapy*, 21 (3): 239–50.

Lambert, M. (1986) In J. Norcross (ed.), *Handbook of Eclectic Psychotherapy*. New York: Brunner/Hazel.

Lankton, S.R. (1990) Ericksonian strategic therapy. In J.K. Zeig and W.W. Munion (eds), *What is Psychotherapy? Contemporary Perspectives*. San Francisco: Jossey-Bass.

Lawson, D. (1994) Identifying pre-treatment change. *Journal of Counselling and Development*, 72: 244–8.

Lazarus, A. (1981) *The Practice of Multimodal Therapy*. New York: McGraw-Hill.

Lethem, J. (1994) *Moved to Tears, Moved to Action. Solution Focused Brief Therapy with Women and Children*. London: Brief Therapy Press.

Lipchik, E. (1991) Spouse abuse: challenging the party line. *The Family Therapy Networker*, 15: 59–63.

Lipchik, E. and de Shazer, S. (1986) The purposeful interview. *Journal of Strategic and Family Therapies*, 5 (1): 88–9.

Lipchik, E. and Kubicki, A.D. (1996) Solution-focused domestic violence views: bridges toward a new reality in couples therapy. In S. Miller, M. Hubble and B. Duncan (eds), *Handbook of Solution Focused Brief Therapy*. San Francisco: Jossey-Bass.

Llewelyn, S.P. (1988) Psychological therapy as viewed by clients and therapists. *British Journal of Clinical Psychology*, 27: 223–37.

Lynch, G. (1996) What is truth? A philosophical introduction to counselling research. *Counselling*, (7) 2: 144–8.

Malan, D.H. (1963) *A Study of Brief Psychotherapy*. New York: Plenum.

Malan, D.H. (1976) *The Frontier of Brief Psychotherapy*. New York: Plenum.

Malan, D., Heath, E., Bacal, H. and Balfour, F. (1975) Psychodynamic changes in untreated neurotic patients. II. Apparently genuine improvements. *Archives of General Psychiatry*, 32: 110–26.

Mann, J. (1973) *Time Limited Psychotherapy*. Cambridge, MA: Harvard University Press.

Manthei, R.J. (1996) A follow up study of clients who fail to begin counselling or terminate after one session. *International Journal for the Advancement of Counselling*, 18: 115–28.

Mason, W.H., Breen, R.Y. and Whipple, W.R. (1994) Solution-focused therapy and inpatient psychiatric nursing. *Nursing*, 32 (10): 46–9.

McConkey, N. (1992) Working with adults to overcome the effects of sexual abuse: integrating solution focused therapy, systems thinking and gender issues. *Journal of Strategic and Systemic Therapies*, 11 (3): 4–18.

McDonald, A.J. (1994) Brief therapy in adult psychiatry, *Journal of Family Therapy*, 16: 415–26.

McKeel, A. and Weiner-Davis, M. (1995) Pre-suppositional questions and pre-treatment change: a further analysis. Unpublished manuscript.

Merl, H. (1995) Reflecting supervision. *Journal of Systemic Therapies*, 14 (2): 47–56.

Merry, T. (1990) Client centred therapy: some trends and some troubles. *Counselling*, 1 (1): 17–18.

Metcalf, L. and Thomas, F. (1994) Client and therapist perceptions of solution focused brief therapy: a qualitative analysis. *Journal of Family Psychotherapy*, (5): 49–66.

Miller, S. (1992) The symptoms of solutions. *Journal of Strategic and Systemic Therapies*, 11 (1): 1–11.

Miller, S. (1994) The solution conspiracy: a mystery in three instalments. *Journal of Systemic Therapies*, 13 (1): 18–37.

Nunnally, E. and Lipchik, E. (1989) Some uses of writing in solution-focused brief therapy. *Journal of Independent Social Work*, 4: 5–19.

Nylund, D. and Corsiglia, V. (1994) Becoming solution-forced in brief therapy: remembering something important we already knew. *Journal of Systemic Therapies*, 13 (1): 5–11.

O'Connell, B. (1997) A grounded theory approach to solution focused therapy. M.Sc. dissertation. Unpublished.

O'Connell, M.F. (1997) Ideas for therapy. Personal communication.

O'Hanlon, B. (1995) Workshop on possibility therapy. London. Organised by the Brief Therapy Practice.

O'Hanlon, B. and Beadle, S. (1994) *A Field Guide to Possibility Land: Possibility Therapy Methods*. Omaha, NE: Possibility Press.

O'Hanlon, B. and Weiner-Davis, M. (1989) *In Search of Solutions*. New York: W.W. Norton.

O'Hanlon, B. and Wilk, J. (1987) *Shifting Contexts*. New York: Guilford Press.

Payne, M. (1993) Down-under innovation: a bridge between person-centred and systemic models. *Counselling*, 4 (2): 117–19.

Pekarik, G. (1991) Relationship of expected and actual treatment duration for adult and child clients. *Journal of Clinical Child Psychology*, 23: 121–5.

Pekarik, G. and Wierzbicki, J. (1986) The relationship between clients' expected and actual treatment duration. *Psychotherapy*, 23: 532–4.

Perry, S. (1987) The choice of duration and frequency for outpatient psychotherapy. *Annual Review*, 6.

Prochaska, J.O., Di Clemente, C.C. and Norcross, J.C. (1992) In search of how people change. *American Psychologist*, 47: 1102–14.

Quick, E. (1994) From unattainable goals to achievable solutions. *Journal of Systemic Therapies*, 13 (2): 59–64.

Rhodes, J. and Ajmal, Y. (1995) *Solution Focused Thinking in Schools*. London: BT Press.

Rilke, R.M. (1990) *Peacemaking: Day by Day, Daily Readings*. London: Pax Christi.

Rogers, C. (1961) *On Becoming a Person*. London: Constable.

Rosenbaum, R., Hoyt, M. and Talmon, M. (1990) The challenge of single session therapies: creating pivotal moments. In R. Wells and V. Gianetti (eds), *The Handbook of Brief Therapies*. New York: Plenum.

Rossi, E. (ed.) (1980) *Collected Papers of Milton Erickson on Hypnosis*. Vol. 4. New York: Irvington.

Russell, R. (1989) Language and psychotherapy. *Clinical Psychology Review*, 9: 505–19.

Ryle, A. (1991) *Cognitive-Analytic Therapy: Active Participation in Change*. Chichester: Wiley.

Schapp, C., Bennun, I., Schindler, L. and Hoogduin, K. (1993) *Therapeutic Relationship in Behavioural Psychotherapy*. Chichester: Wiley.

Schwartz, D.P. (1955) Has family therapy reached the stage where it can appreciate the concept of stages? In J. Breunlin (ed.), *Stages: Patterns of Change over Time*. Rockville, MA: Aspen.

Segal, L. (1986) *The Dream of Reality: Heinz Von Foerster's Constructivism*. New York: W.W. Norton.

Selekman, M. (1991) The solution-oriented parenting group: a treatment alternative that works. *Journal of Strategic and Systemic Therapies*, 10 (1): 36–48.

Selekman, M. and Todd, T. (1995) Co-creating a context for change in the supervisory system: the solution focused supervision model. *Journal of Systemic Therapies*, 14 (3): 21–33.

Sifneos, P.E. (1979) *Short Term Dynamic Psychotherapy*. New York: Plenum.

Skott-Myhre, H. (1992) *Competency Based Counseling, Basic Principles and Assumptions*. Santa Fe: Further Institute Press.

Slive, A., MacLaurin, B., Oakander, M. and Amundson, J. (1995) Walk-in single sessions: a new paradigm in clinical service delivery. *Journal of Systemic Therapies*, 14 (1): 3–11.

Smith, M.L. (1980) *The Benefits of Psychotherapy*. Baltimore: Johns Hopkins University.

Steenbarger, B. (1994) Toward science – practice integration in brief counselling and therapy. *The Counseling Psychologist*, 20 (3): 403–50.

Stern, S. (1993) Managed care, brief therapy, and therapeutic integrity. *Psychotherapy*, 30 (1): 162–75.

Street, E. and Downey, J. (1996) *Brief Therapeutic Consultations*. Chichester: Wiley.

Talmon, M. (1990) *Single Session Therapy*. San Francisco: Jossey-Bass.

Talmon, M. (1996) Presentation on single session therapy. London. Organised by the Brief Therapy Practice.

Taylor, C. (1985) Theories of meaning. In C. Taylor (ed.), *Human Agency and Language*. Cambridge: Cambridge University Press.

Thomas, F. (1994) Solution-oriented supervision: the coaxing of expertise. *The Family Journal*, 2 (1): 11–17.

Ticho, E.A. (1972) Termination of psychoanalysis: treatment goals and life goals. *Psychoanalysis Quarterly*, 41: 315–33.

Twyn, L. (1992) Solution-oriented therapy and Rogerian Nursing Science: an integrated approach. *Archives in Psychiatric Nursing*, 6 (2): 83–9.

Vaughn, K., Hastings, G. and Kassner, C. (1996) Solution-oriented inpatient group therapy. *Journal of Systemic Therapies*, 15 (3): 1–14.

Vaughn, K., Cox Young, B., Webster, D.C. and Thomas, M.R. (1996) Solution-focused work in the hospital. In S. Miller, M. Hubble and B. Duncan (eds), *Handbook of Solution Focused Brief Therapy*. San Francisco: Jossey-Bass.

Walter, J. and Peller, J. (1996) Assuming anew in a postmodern world. In S. Miller, M. Hubble and B. Duncan (eds), *Handbook of Solution Focused Brief Therapy*. San Francisco: Jossey-Bass.

Warner, R.E. (1996) Counsellor bias against short term counselling. A comparison of counsellor and client satisfaction in a Canadian setting. *International Journal for the Advancement of Counselling*, 18: 153–62.

Washburn, P. (1994) Advantages of a brief solution oriented focus in home based family preservation services. *Journal of Systemic Therapies*, 13 (2): 47–58.

Watzlawick, P. (1984) *The Invented Reality*. New York: W.W. Norton.

Watzlawick, P., Weakland, J. and Fisch, R. (1974) *Change: Principles of Problem Formation and Problem Resolution*. New York: W.W. Norton.

Weakland, J., Fisch, R., Watzlawick, P. and Bodin, A. (1974) Brief therapy: focused problem resolution. *Family Process*, 13: 141–68.

Weakland, J. and Jordan, L. (1992) Working briefly with reluctant clients: child protective services as an example. *Journal of Family Therapy*, 14: 231–54.

Webster, D. (1990) Solution-focused approaches in psychiatric/mental health nursing. *Perspectives in Psychiatric Care*, 26 (4): 17–21.

Weiner-Davis, M., de Shazer, S. and Gingerich, W. (1987) Building on pre-treatment change to construct the therapeutic solution: an exploratory study. *Journal of Marital and Family Therapy*, 13 (4): 359–63.

Wells, R. and Gianetti, V. (eds) (1993) *Casebook of the Brief Psychotherapies*. New York: Plenum Press.

Wetchler, J.L. (1990) Solution-focused supervision. *Family Therapy*, 17 (2): 129–38.

White, M. (1988) The process of questioning: A therapy of literary merit? *Dulwich Newsletter*, Summer: 3–21.

White, M. (1989) *Selected Papers*. Adelaide: Dulwich Centre Publications.

White, M. (1993) Deconstruction and therapy. In S. Gilligan and R. Price (eds), *Therapeutic Conversations*. New York: W.W. Norton. pp 22–62.

White, M. (1995) *Re-Authoring Lives: Interviews and Essays*. Adelaide: Dulwich Centre Publications.

White, M. and Epston, D. (1990) *Narrative Means to Therapeutic Ends*. New York: W.W. Norton.

Widdicombe, S. (1993) Autobiography and change: rhetoric and authenticity of 'Gothic' style. In E. Burman and I. Parker (eds), *Discourse Analysis Research*. London: Routledge.

Wilgosh, R. (1993) How can we see where we're going if we're always looking backwards? *Counselling*, 4 (2): 98–101.

Wilkins, P. (1993) Person-centred therapy and the person-centred approach: a personal view. *Counselling*, 4 (1): 31–2.

Zimmerman, T.S., Prest, L.A. and Wetzel, B.E. (1997) Solution-focused couples therapy groups: an empirical study. *Journal of Family Therapy*, 19: 125–44.

Author Index

Subject Index

References to boxed material appear in italics.